JESUS

ALSO BY MAX LUCADO

INSPIRATIONAL

3:16
A Gentle Thunder
A Love Worth Giving
And the Angels Were Silent
Anxious for Nothing
Because of Bethlehem
Before Amen
Come Thirsty
Cure for the Common Life
Facing Your Giants
Fearless
Glory Days
God Came Near
Grace
Great Day Every Day
He Chose the Nails
He Still Moves Stones
How Happiness Happens
In the Eye of the Storm
In the Grip of Grace
It's Not About Me
Just Like Jesus
Max on Life
More to Your Story
Next Door Savior
No Wonder They Call Him the Savior
On the Anvil
Outlive Your Life
Six Hours One Friday
The Applause of Heaven
The Great House of God
Traveling Light
Unshakable Hope
When Christ Comes
When God Whispers Your Name
You'll Get Through This

FICTION

Christmas Stories
Miracle at the Higher Grounds Café
The Christmas Candle

BIBLES (GENERAL EDITOR)

Children's Daily Devotional Bible
Grace for the Moment Daily Bible
The Lucado Life Lessons Study Bible

CHILDREN'S BOOKS

A Max Lucado Children's Treasury
Do You Know I Love You, God?
God Always Keeps His Promises
God Forgives Me, and I Forgive You
God Listens When I Pray
Grace for the Moment: 365
Devotions for Kids
Hermie, a Common Caterpillar
I'm Not a Scaredy Cat
Itsy Bitsy Christmas
Just in Case You Ever Wonder
Lucado Treasury of Bedtime Prayers
One Hand, Two Hands
Thank You, God, for Blessing Me
Thank You, God, for Loving Me
The Boy and the Ocean
The Crippled Lamb
The Oak Inside the Acorn
The Tallest of Smalls
You Are Mine
You Are Special

YOUNG ADULT BOOKS

3:16
It's Not About Me
Make Every Day Count
Wild Grace
You Were Made to Make a Difference

GIFT BOOKS

Fear Not Promise Book
For the Tough Times
God Thinks You're Wonderful
Grace for the Moment
Grace Happens Here
Happy Today
His Name Is Jesus
Let the Journey Begin
Live Loved
Mocha with Max
Safe in the Shepherd's Arms
This Is Love
You Changed My Life

JESUS

*The God Who Knows
Your Name*

MAX LUCADO

THOMAS NELSON
Since 1798

Published in Nashville, Tennessee, by Nelson Books, an imprint of Thomas Nelson. Nelson Books and Thomas Nelson are registered trademarks of HarperCollins Christian Publishing, Inc.

Thomas Nelson titles may be purchased in bulk for educational, business, fund-raising, or sales promotional use. For information, please e-mail SpecialMarkets@ThomasNelson.com.

Unless otherwise noted, Scripture quotations are taken from the Holy Bible, New International Version®, NIV®. Copyright © 1973, 1978, 1984, 2011 by Biblica, Inc.® Used by permission of Zondervan. All rights reserved worldwide. www.Zondervan.com. The "NIV" and "New International Version" are trademarks registered in the United States Patent and Trademark Office by Biblica, Inc.® Scripture quotations marked AMP are from the Amplified® Bible. Copyright © 1954, 1958, 1962, 1964, 1965, 1987 by The Lockman Foundation. Used by permission. (www.Lockman.org) Scripture quotations marked CEB are from the Common English Bible. Copyright © 2011 Common English Bible. Scripture quotations marked CEV are from the Contemporary English Version. Copyright © 1991, 1992, 1995 by American Bible Society. Used by permission. Scripture quotations marked ESV are from the ESV® Bible (The Holy Bible, English Standard Version®). Copyright © 2001 by Crossway, a publishing ministry of Good News Publishers. Used by permission. All rights reserved. Scripture quotations marked GNT are from the Good News Translation in Today's English Version—Second Edition. Copyright © 1992 by American Bible Society. Used by permission. Scripture quotations marked GW are from God's Word®. Copyright © 1995 God's Word to the Nations. Used by permission of Baker Publishing Group. All rights reserved. Scripture quotations marked KJV are from the King James Version. Public domain. Scripture quotations marked THE MESSAGE are from The Message. Copyright © by Eugene H. Peterson 1993, 1994, 1995, 1996, 2000, 2001, 2002. Used by permission of NavPress. All rights reserved. Represented by Tyndale House Publishers, Inc. Scripture quotations marked NABRE are from New American Bible, revised edition. © 1970, 1986, 1991, 2010, Confraternity of Christian Doctrine, Inc., Washington, DC. All rights reserved. Scripture quotations marked NASB are from New American Standard Bible®. Copyright © 1960, 1962, 1963, 1968, 1971, 1972, 1973, 1975, 1977, 1995 by The Lockman Foundation. Used by permission. (www.Lockman.org) Scripture quotations marked NCV are from the New Century Version®. © 2005 by Thomas Nelson. Used by permission. All rights reserved. Scripture quotations marked NEB are from the New English Bible. © Cambridge University Press and Oxford University Press 1961, 1970. All rights reserved. Scripture quotations marked NKJV are from the New King James Version®. © 1982 by Thomas Nelson. Used by permission. All rights reserved. Scripture quotations marked NLT are from the Holy Bible, New Living Translation. © 1996, 2004, 2007, 2013, 2015 by Tyndale House Foundation. Used by permission of Tyndale House Publishers, Inc., Carol Stream, Illinois 60188. All rights reserved. Scripture quotations marked NRSV are from New Revised Standard Version Bible. Copyright © 1989 National Council of the Churches of Christ in the United States of America. Used by permission. All rights reserved. Scripture quotations marked PHILLIPS are from The New Testament in Modern English by J. B. Phillips. Copyright © 1960, 1972 J. B. Phillips. Administered by the Archbishops' Council of the Church of England. Used by permission. Scripture quotations marked RSV are from Revised Standard Version of the Bible. Copyright 1946, 1952, and 1971 National Council of the Churches of Christ in the United States of America. Used by permission. All rights reserved. Scripture quotations marked THE VOICE are from The Voice™. © 2012 by Ecclesia Bible Society. Used by permission. All rights reserved. Note: Italics in quotations from The Voice are used to "indicate words not directly tied to the dynamic translation of the original language" but that "bring out the nuance of the original, assist in completing ideas, and . . . provide readers with information that would have been obvious to the original audience" (The Voice, preface).

ISBN 978-1-4002-1470-9 (eBook)
ISBN 978-1-4002-1469-3 (HC)
ISBN 978-1-4002-1472-3 (TP)
ISBN 978-1-4002-1695-6 (IE)

Library of Congress Cataloging-in-Publication Data

Names: Lucado, Max, author.
Title: Jesus / Max Lucado.
Description: Nashville : Thomas Nelson, 2019. | Originally published: 2018.
| Includes bibliographical references. | Summary: "Beloved pastor and bestselling author Max Lucado explores the life and character of Jesus, offering readers a chance to become more familiar with the man at the center of the greatest story ever told-a story that includes each of us!"-- Provided by publisher.
Identifiers: LCCN 2019027088 (print) | LCCN 2019027089 (ebook) | ISBN 9781400214693 (hardcover) | ISBN 9781400214709 (ebook)
Subjects: LCSH: Jesus Christ--Person and offices..
Classification: LCC BT203 .L835 2019 (print) | LCC BT203 (ebook) | DDC 232.9--dc23
LC record available at https://lccn.loc.gov/2019027088
LC ebook record available at https://lccn.loc.gov/2019027089

Printed in the United States of America
20 21 22 23 24 LSC 10 9 8 7 6 5 4 3 2 1

Denalyn and I joyfully dedicate this volume
to our son-in-law Jeff Jones.
Everyone who knows you is a better person because they do.
Thanks for loving our girl! We sure love you.

Contents

CONTENTS

TEACHER

MIRACLE WORKER

LAMB OF GOD

RETURNING KING

Acknowledgments

I want to thank my good friends at HarperCollins Christian Publishing for their incredible support. Mark Schoenwald, David Moberg, Brian Hampton, Janene MacIvor, Jessalyn Foggy, and Mark Glesne championed this project from start to finish. Add to that list the names of our publishing team: Karen Hill, Steve and Cheryl Green, Greg and Susan Ligon. My daughter Andrea Lucado provided excellent editorial support. And Carol Bartley, every author's dream come true, applied her copyediting skills. All in all, it was a gigantic team effort.

Introduction

Carinette has a spark in her. A look. A bounce in her step. A light in her eyes. She is one of fifty-seven children in the Haitian orphanage: all dark skinned, bright eyed, curly haired, Creole speaking, and fun loving. Each one is precious. But this seven-year-old stands out from the others. Not as a result of special treatment. She eats the same rice and beans as the others eat and plays on the same grassless playground. She sleeps beneath the same tin roof as the other girls, hearing the nearly nightly pound of rain. Her routine is identical to the other children's. Yet she is different.

The reason? Ask her. Ask Carinette about the visitors who traveled from a faraway world just to see her. They were looking for a girl, a little girl, a girl just like her. They knew her name. They knew her favorite song. They knew that she loves to look at books and jump rope. And, in a moment that changed her forever, they invited her to live with them.

"They are coming for me," she will tell you.

Ask to see the pictures of her soon-to-be home; she'll show them to you. Fail to ask; she'll offer to show you. Her adoptive parents brought her pictures, a teddy bear, granola bars, and cookies. She shared the goodies with her friends and asked the director to guard her bear, but she keeps the pictures.

They remind her of the father who knows her. They remind her of the home that awaits her. The photographs convince her to believe the incredible: somebody knows her name and has promised to take her home.

As a result Carinette is different. She still lives in the same orphanage, plays on the same playground, eats in the same cafeteria. But her world changed the day she learned that someone faraway knows her name and is coming for her.

Might you be willing to believe the same?

Are you open to the idea of a Father, a heavenly Father, who knows you? A soon-to-be home that awaits you? Would you consider this life-changing idea: the almighty and all-knowing God has set his affection on you. Every detail about you he knows. Your interests, your hang-ups. Your fears and failures. He knows you.

About his children God says, "The LORD searches every heart and understands every desire and every thought" (1 Chron. 28:9).

He regards you as "the apple of his eye" (Zech. 2:8).

He can "sympathize with our weaknesses" (Heb. 4:15 NKJV).

"When my spirit was overwhelmed within me . . . ," King David wrote, "You knew my path" (Ps. 142:3 NKJV).

"He knows the way that I take," declared Job (Job 23:10 NKJV).

Do you know this God who knows you?

He knows your name. And he can't wait to get you home.

I came to know the story of the Cap-Haïtien orphan, not by traveling to Haiti, but by standing in the church foyer. I'm a pastor. Like other pastors I like to greet people after church services. And like other pastors I am a captive audience for parents and grandparents who want to show off new additions to the family. I've held more babies than I can count and looked at more pictures than a photographer. But I can't recall ever being more surprised than the day Dan wanted to show me a photo of his new daughter.

The girl in the photo smiled a big smile, wore a pink ribbon, and had skin the color of chocolate.

The guy who handed me the photo smiled a big smile, wore cowboy boots and a hat, and had skin the color of Casper the Friendly Ghost.

"Daughter?"

That's when I heard about the orphanage, the trip, and the decision to expand their family by adding one more face around the table. He scarcely took a breath for the next five minutes, telling me all about her hair, eyes, and favorite color, song, and book. He couldn't stop talking about her. He was crazy about her.

Might you believe the same about your Father?

This is the ever-recurring, soul-lifting message of heaven.

"The LORD delights in you" (Isa. 62:4 NKJV).

"Fear not, for I have redeemed you; I have called you by your name; You are Mine" (Isa. 43:1 NKJV).

"I have written your name on the palms of my hands" (Isa. 49:16 NLT).

"The LORD takes pleasure in those who fear Him, in those who hope in His mercy" (Ps. 147:11 NKJV).

"The LORD directs the steps of the godly. He delights in every detail of their lives. Though they stumble, they will never fall, for the LORD holds them by the hand" (Ps. 37:23–24 NLT).

Do such words surprise you? Where did we get this idea of a God who does not care, who is not near? We certainly didn't get it from Jesus.

Jesus Christ is the perfect picture of God. Just as Carinette had her photos, we have Jesus. Want to know how God feels about the sick? Look at Jesus. What angers God? Look at Jesus. Does God ever give up on people? Does he stand up for people? Find the answer in Jesus. "The Son is the radiance and only expression of the glory of [our awesome] God . . . and the exact representation and perfect imprint of His [Father's] essence" (Heb. 1:3 AMP).

The pictures inform Carinette's thoughts about her home-to-be. She's not home yet. Within a month she will be, maybe. Two at the most. She knows the day is coming. She knows the hour is imminent. Every opening of the gate makes her heart jump. Any day now her father will appear. He's coming. He promised he'd be back. He came once to claim her. He'll come again to carry her.

Till then she lives with a heart headed home.

Shouldn't we all? Carinette's situation mirrors ours. Have we not been claimed? Are we not adopted children? "So you have not received a spirit that makes you fearful slaves. Instead, you received God's Spirit when he adopted you as his own children. Now we call him, 'Abba, Father'" (Rom. 8:15 NLT).

God sought you. He searched you out. Before you knew you needed adopting, he'd already filed the papers.

"For God knew his people in advance, and he chose them to become like his Son, so that his Son would be the firstborn among many brothers and sisters" (Rom. 8:29 NLT).

Abandon you to a fatherless world of tin plates and hard bunks? No way. Those privy to God's family Bible can read your name. He put your name in his book. What's more, he covered the adoption fees. "God sent him [Christ] to buy freedom for us who were slaves to the law, so that he could adopt us as his very own children" (Gal. 4:5 NLT).

We don't finance our adoption, but we do accept it. Carinette could tell the Johnsons to get lost. But she didn't. You can tell God to get lost. But you wouldn't dare, would you? "You are all children of God through faith in Christ Jesus" (Gal. 3:26 NLT). The moment we accept his offer we go from orphans to heirs: "You are his heirs . . ." (Gal. 3:29 NLT).

Heirs! Heirs with a new name. New home. New life. "Heirs of God and joint heirs with Christ" (Rom. 8:17 NKJV). Heaven knows no stepchildren or grandchildren. You and Christ share the same will. What he inherits, you inherit. You are headed home.

Oh, but we tend to forget, don't we? We grow accustomed to hard bunks and crowded classrooms. Too seldom do we peer over the fence into the world to come. And how long since you pictured your future home? Is Peter speaking to us when he urges, "Friends, this world is not your home, so don't make yourselves cozy in it" (1 Peter 2:11 THE MESSAGE)?

Like Carinette we are adopted but not transported. We have a new family but haven't met all of them yet. We know our Father's name, and he has claimed us, but he has yet to come for us.

So here we are. Caught between what is and what will be. No longer orphans but not yet home. What do we do in the meantime? Indeed, it can be just that—a mean time. Time made mean with disease, deceit, death, and debt. How do we live in the meantime? How do we keep our hearts headed home?

"Let us look only to Jesus, the One who began our faith and who makes it perfect" (Heb. 12:2 NCV).

Look to Jesus. Ponder his life. Consider his ways. Meditate on his words. Jesus. Just Jesus.

That is the aim of this book that you hold. It contains both published and heretofore unpublished thoughts about the life of Christ. With these words may I offer this prayer:

May the Hero of all history talk personally to you. May you find in Jesus the answer to the deepest needs of your life. May you remember your highest privilege: you are known by God and cherished by heaven.

Keep an eye on the front gate. Your Father will show up to take you home before you know it.

PART 1

IMMANUEL

When our daughter Sara was four years old, she burst into the house carrying a water-filled baggie in which swam a wide-eyed burst of sunshine. "Look what they gave us at the birthday party!" (Gee thanks.) We dumped the pet into a fishbowl and gathered around to select a name. *Sebastian* won. He quickly became the star of the family. We actually set the bowl on the dinner table so we could watch him swim while we ate. The ultimate fish dinner.

But then we got bored. Can't fault Sebastian. He did everything expected of a family fish. He swam in circles and surfaced on cue to gobble fish food. He never jumped out of the bowl into the sink or demanded a seat on the couch. He spent his nights nestled amid a green plant. Quiet. Novel. Contained. Like Jesus?

The Jesus of many people is small enough to be contained in an aquarium that fits on the cabinet. Package him up, and send him home with the kids. Dump him in a bowl, and watch him swim. He never causes trouble or demands attention. Everyone wants a goldfish bowl of Jesus, right? If you do, steer clear of the real Jesus Christ. He brings a wild ride. He comes at you like a fire hose—blasting, purging, cleansing. He will not swim quietly. He is more

3

a force than a fixture, flushing away every last clod of doubt and death and infusing us with wonder and hope.

He changes everything. Jesus does not promise to stop your snoring, turn your kids into valedictorians, or guarantee you will have the correct lottery number. Jesus doesn't make you sexy, skinny, or clever. Jesus doesn't change what you see in the mirror. He changes how you see what you see.

He will not be silenced, packaged, or predicted. He is the pastor who chased people out of church. He is the prophet who had a soft spot for crooks and whores. He is the king who washed the grime off the feet of his betrayer. He turned a bread basket into a buffet and a dead friend into a living one. And most of all, he transformed the tomb into a womb out of which life was born. Your life.

Jesus: Five letters. Six hours. One cross. Three nails. We live because he does, hope because he works, and matter because he matters. To be saved by grace is to be saved by him—not by an idea, doctrine, creed, or church membership, but by Jesus himself, who will sweep into heaven anyone who so much as gives him the nod.

Goldfish Jesus? Not on your life.

Goldfish Jesus happens only on Christmas and Easter. The real Jesus claims every tick of the clock.

Goldfish Jesus winks at sin. The real Jesus nukes it.

Goldfish Jesus is a lucky charm crucifix on a necklace. Jesus is a tiger in your heart.

Do you know this Jesus? If your answer is no, let's talk about him. If your answer is yes, let's talk about him. Let's talk about Jesus.

Let's begin where the earthly ministry of Jesus began—in the

---

womb of Mary. The God of the universe, for a time, kicked against the wall of that womb. He was born in the poverty of a peasant and spent his first night in the feed trough of a cow. "The Word became flesh and blood, and moved into the neighborhood" (John 1:14 THE MESSAGE).

Didn't have to, did he?

Jesus could have become a voice—a voice in the air.

Jesus could have become a message—a message in the sky.

Jesus could have become a light—a light in the night.

But he became more, so much more. He became flesh. Why? Why did he take the journey? Why did he go so far?

Might the answer include this word: *you*?

Jesus came to be near you. Any concerns you might have about his power and love were removed from the discussion the moment he became flesh and entered the world.

What a beginning. What an entrance. What a moment. Goldfish Jesus? No way.

Chapter 1

Born to You This Day

Born to a mother.
Acquainted with physical pain.
Enjoys a good party.
Rejected by friends.
Unfairly accused.
Loves stories.
Reluctantly pays taxes.
Sings.
Turned off by greedy religion.
Feels sorry for the lonely.
Unappreciated by siblings.

Stands up for the underdog.
Kept awake at night by concerns.
Known to doze off in the midst of trips.
Accused of being too rowdy.
Afraid of death.

Whom am I describing? Jesus . . . or you? Perhaps both.

Based on this list, it seems you and I have a lot in common with Jesus.

Big deal? I think so.

Jesus understands you. He understands small-town anonymity and big-city pressure. He's walked through pastures of sheep and palaces of kings. He's faced hunger, sorrow, and death and wants to face them with you. Jesus "understands our weaknesses, for he faced all of the same testings we do, yet he did not sin" (Heb. 4:15 NLT).

If Jesus understands our weaknesses, then so does God. Jesus was God in human form. He was God with us. That is why Jesus is called Immanuel.

Immanuel appears in the same Hebrew form as it did two thousand years ago. *Immanu* means "with us." *El* refers to *Elohim,* or God. So Immanuel is not an "above-us God" or a "somewhere-in-the-neighborhood God." He came as the "with-us God." God with us. Not "God with the rich" or "God with the religious." But God with *us.* All of us. Russians, Germans, Buddhists, Mormons, truck drivers and taxi drivers, librarians. God with *us.*

Don't we love the word *with*? "Will you go *with* me?" we ask. "To the store, to the hospital, through my life?" God says he will.

"I am *with* you always," Jesus said before he ascended to heaven, "to the very end of the age" (Matt. 28:20). Search for restrictions on the promise; you'll find none. You won't find "I'll be with you if you behave . . . when you believe. I'll be with you on Sundays in worship . . . at mass." No, none of that. There's no withholding tax on God's "with" promise. He is *with* us.

God is with us.

Prophets weren't enough. Apostles wouldn't do. Angels won't suffice. God sent more than miracles and messages. He sent himself; he sent his Son. "The Word became flesh and dwelt among us" (John 1:14 NKJV).

For thousands of years God gave us his voice. Prior to Bethlehem he gave us his messengers, his teachers, his words. But in the manger God gave us himself. Extraordinary, don't you think?

I imagine even Gabriel scratched his head at the idea of "God with us." Gabriel wasn't one to question his God-given missions. Sending fire and dividing seas were all in an eternity's work for this angel. When God sent, Gabriel went.

And when word got out that God was to become a human, Gabriel was no doubt enthused. He could envision the moment:

The Messiah in a blazing chariot.

The King descending on a fiery cloud.

An explosion of light from which the Messiah would emerge.

That's surely what he expected. What he never expected, however, was what he got: a slip of paper with a Nazarene address. "God will become a baby," it read. "Tell the mother to name the child *Jesus*. And tell her not to be afraid."

Gabriel was never one to question, but this time he had to

wonder. *God will become a baby?* Gabriel had seen babies before. He had been platoon leader on the bulrush operation. He remembered what little Moses looked like.

That's okay for humans, he thought to himself. *But for God? The heavens can't contain him. How could a body? Besides, have you seen what comes out of those babies? Hardly befitting the Creator of the universe. Babies must be carried and fed, bounced and bathed. Some mother burping God on her shoulder?* Why, that was beyond what even an angel could imagine.

And what of this name? What was it—Jesus? Such a common name. There's a Jesus in every cul-de-sac. Come on, even the name Gabriel has more punch to it than Jesus. *Call the baby Eminence or Majesty or Heaven-sent. Anything but Jesus.*

So Gabriel scratched his head. *What happened to the good ol' days?* Global floods. Flaming swords. That's the action he liked.

But Gabriel had his orders. Take the message to Mary. *Must be a special girl*, he assumed as he traveled. But Gabriel was in for another shock. One peek told him Mary was no queen. The mother-to-be of God was not regal. She was a Jewish peasant who'd barely outgrown her acne and had a crush on a guy named Joe.

And speaking of Joe, what does this fellow know? Might as well be a weaver in Spain or a cobbler in Greece. He's a carpenter. Look at him over there—sawdust in his beard and a nail apron around his waist. You're telling me that God is going to have dinner every night with him? You're telling me that the source of wisdom is going to call this guy "Dad"? You're telling me that a common laborer is going to be charged with providing food to God?

What if he gets laid off?

What if he gets cranky?

What if he decides to run off with a pretty young girl from down the street? Then where will we be?

It was all Gabriel could do to keep from turning back. "This is a peculiar idea you have, God," he must have muttered to himself, but he followed through. He wasn't about to rebel against his boss, who also happened to control the universe.

He visited Mary and told her:

> Do not be afraid, Mary, for you have found favor with God. And behold, you will conceive in your womb and bring forth a Son, and shall call His name JESUS. (Luke 1:30–31 NKJV)

The story of Jesus begins with the story of a great descent. The Son of God became the child of Mary. He became one of us so we might become one with Him. He entered our world in the high hope that we will enter his.

———

Chapter 2

No Ordinary Night

Only one word describes the night he finally came—*ordinary*.
The sky was ordinary. An occasional gust stirred the leaves and chilled the air. The stars were diamonds sparkling on black velvet. Fleets of clouds floated in front of the moon.

It was a beautiful night—a night worth peeking out your bedroom window to admire—but not really an unusual one. No reason to expect a surprise. Nothing to keep a person awake. An ordinary night with an ordinary sky.

The sheep were ordinary. Some fat. Some scrawny. Some with barrel bellies. Some with twig legs. Common animals. No fleece made of gold. No history makers. No blue-ribbon winners. They were simply sheep—lumpy, sleeping silhouettes on a hillside.

And the shepherds. Peasants they were. Probably wearing all the clothes they owned. Smelling like sheep and looking just as woolly. They were conscientious, willing to spend the night with their flocks. But you won't find their staffs in a museum or their writings in a library. No one asked their opinion on social justice or the application of the Torah. They were nameless and simple.

An ordinary night with ordinary sheep and ordinary shepherds. And were it not for a God who loves to hook an *extra* on the front of the ordinary, the night would have gone unnoticed.

But God dances amid the common. And that night he did a waltz.

The black sky exploded with brightness. Trees that had been shadows jumped into clarity. Sheep that had been silent became a chorus of curiosity. One minute the shepherd was dead asleep. The next he was rubbing his eyes and staring into the face of an angel, who declared, "There is born to you this day in the city of David a Savior, who is Christ the Lord" (Luke 2:11 NKJV).

The night was ordinary no more.

As dark gave way to dawn, the noise and the bustle began earlier than usual in the village of Bethlehem. People were already on the streets. Vendors were positioning themselves on the corners of the most heavily traveled avenues. Store owners were unlocking the doors to their shops. Children were awakened by the excited barking of the street dogs and the complaints of donkeys pulling carts.

The owner of the inn had awakened earlier than most in the town. After all, the inn was full, all the beds taken. Every available mat or blanket had been put to use. Soon all the customers would be stirring, and there would be a lot of work to do.

One's imagination is kindled, thinking about the conversation of the innkeeper and his family at the breakfast table. Did anyone mention the arrival of the young couple the night before? Did anyone ask about their welfare? Did anyone comment on the pregnancy of the girl on the donkey? Perhaps. Perhaps someone raised the subject. But, at best, it was raised, not discussed. There was nothing novel about them. They were possibly one of several families turned away that night.

Besides, who had time to talk about them when there was so much excitement in the air? Augustus did the economy of Bethlehem a favor when he decreed that a census should be taken and people should return to their hometowns. Who could remember when such commerce had hit the village?

No, it is doubtful that anyone mentioned the couple's arrival or wondered about the condition of the girl. They were too busy. The day was upon them. The day's bread had to be made. The morning's chores had to be done. There was too much to do to imagine that the impossible had occurred.

God had entered the world as a baby.

Yet were someone to chance upon the sheep stable on the outskirts of Bethlehem that morning, what a peculiar scene they would behold.

The stable stinks as all stables do. The stench of urine, dung, and sheep reeks pungently in the air. The ground is hard, the hay scarce. Cobwebs cling to the ceiling, and a mouse scurries across the dirt floor.

A more lowly place of birth could not exist.

Off to one side is a group of shepherds. They sit silently on the floor, perhaps perplexed, perhaps in awe, no doubt in amazement. Their night watch had been interrupted by an explosion of light from heaven and a symphony of angels. God goes to those who have time to hear him, so on this cloudless night he went to simple shepherds.

Near the young mother sits the weary father. If anyone is dozing, he is. He can't remember the last time he sat down. And now that the excitement has subsided a bit, now that Mary and the baby are comfortable, he leans against the wall of the stable and feels his eyes grow heavy. He still hasn't figured it all out. The mystery of the event puzzles him. But he hasn't the energy to wrestle with the questions. What's important is that the baby is fine and Mary is safe. As sleep comes, he remembers the name the angel told him to use—*Jesus*. "We will call him Jesus."

Mary is wide awake. My, how young she looks! Her head rests on the soft leather of Joseph's saddle. The pain has been eclipsed by wonder. She looks into the face of the baby. Her son. Her Lord. His Majesty. At this point in history the human being who best understands who God is and what he is doing is a teenage girl in a smelly stable. She can't take her eyes off him. Somehow Mary knows she is holding God. *So this is he.* She remembers the words of the angel: "His kingdom will never end" (Luke 1:33).

He looks like anything but a king. His face is prunish and red. His cry, though strong and healthy, is still the helpless and piercing cry of a baby. And he is absolutely dependent on Mary for his well-being.

Majesty in the midst of the mundane. Holiness in the filth of sheep manure and sweat. Divinity entering the world on the floor of a stable, through the womb of a teenager, and in the presence of a carpenter.

She touches the face of the infant God. *How long was your journey!*

This baby had overseen the universe. His golden throne room had been abandoned in favor of a dirty sheep pen. And worshiping angels had been exchanged for kind but bewildered shepherds.

God's nature would not hold him in heaven. It led him to earth. In God's great gospel he not only sends, but he also becomes; he not only looks down, but he also lives among; he not only talks to us, but he also lives with us as one of us.

God with us.

Chapter 3

The Word Became Flesh

D o you know the most remarkable part of the incarnation?
Not just that God swapped eternity for calendars, though
such an exchange deserves our notice.

Scripture says that the number of God's years is unsearchable
(Job 36:26 NASB). We may search out the moment the first wave
slapped on a shore or the first star burst in the sky, but we'll never
find the first moment when God was God, for there is no moment
when God was not God. He has never not been, for he is eternal.
God is not bound by time.

But when Jesus came to the earth, all this changed. He heard
for the first time a phrase never used in heaven: "Your time is up."
As a child he had to leave the temple because his time was up. As

a man he had to leave Nazareth because his time was up. And as a Savior he had to die because his time was up. For thirty-three years the stallion of heaven lived in the corral of time.

That's certainly remarkable, but there is something even more so.

Do you want to see the brightest jewel in the treasure of the incarnation? You might think it was the fact that he lived in a body. One moment he was a boundless spirit; the next he was flesh and bones. Do you remember these words of King David: "Where can I go to get away from your Spirit? Where can I run from you? If I go up to the heavens, you are there. If I lie down in the grave, you are there. If I rise with the sun in the east and settle in the west beyond the sea, even there you would guide me" (Ps. 139:7–10 NCV)?

Our asking "Where is God?" is like a fish asking "Where is water?" or a bird asking "Where is air?" God is everywhere! Equally present in Peking and Peoria. As active in the lives of Icelanders as in the lives of Texans. The dominion of God is "from sea to sea and from the River to the ends of the earth" (Ps. 72:8). We cannot find a place where God is not.

Yet when God entered time and became a man, he who was boundless became bound. Imprisoned in flesh. Restricted by weary-prone muscles and droopy eyelids. For more than three decades his once-limitless reach would be limited to the stretch of an arm, his speed checked to the pace of human feet.

I wonder, Was he ever tempted to reclaim his boundlessness? In the middle of a long trip, did he ever consider transporting himself to the next city? When the rain chilled his bones, was he tempted to change the weather? When the heat parched his lips, did he give thought to popping over to the Caribbean for some refreshment?

———

If ever he entertained such thoughts, he never gave in to them. Not once. Stop and think about this. Not once did Christ use his supernatural powers for personal comfort. With one word he could've transformed the hard earth into a soft bed, but he didn't. With a wave of his hand, he could've boomeranged the spit of his accusers back into their faces, but he didn't. With an arch of his brow, he could've paralyzed the hand of the soldier as he braided the crown of thorns. But he didn't.

Remarkable. But is this the most remarkable part of the coming? Many would argue not. Many, perhaps most, would point beyond the surrender of timelessness and boundlessness to the surrender of sinlessness. It's easy to see why.

Isn't this the message of the crown of thorns?

An unnamed soldier took branches—mature enough to bear thorns, nimble enough to bend—and wove them into a crown of mockery, a crown of thorns.

Throughout Scripture thorns symbolize, not sin, but the consequence of sin. Remember Eden? After Adam and Eve sinned, God cursed the land: "So I will put a curse on the ground. . . . The ground will produce thorns and weeds for you, and you will eat the plants of the field" (Gen. 3:17–18 NCV). Brambles on the earth are the product of sin in the heart.

What is the fruit of sin? Step into the briar patch of humanity and feel a few thistles. Shame. Fear. Disgrace. Discouragement. Anxiety. Haven't our hearts been caught in these brambles?

The heart of Jesus, however, had not. He had never been cut by the thorns of sin. What you and I face daily, he never knew. Anxiety? He never worried! Guilt? He was never guilty! Fear? He never left the presence of God! Jesus never knew the fruits of sin . . . until he became sin for us.

And when he did, all the emotions of sin tumbled in on him like the waves of a stormy sea. He felt anxious, guilty, and alone. Can't you hear the emotion in his prayer? "My God, my God, why have you abandoned me?" (Matt. 27:46 NCV). These are not the words of a saint. This is the cry of a sinner.

And this prayer is one of the most remarkable parts of his coming. But I can think of something even greater. Want to know what it is? Want to know the coolest thing about the coming?

Not that the One who played marbles with the stars gave it up to play marbles with marbles. Or that the One who hung the galaxies gave it up to hang doorjambs to the displeasure of a cranky client who wanted everything yesterday but couldn't pay for anything until tomorrow.

Not that he in an instant went from needing nothing to needing air, food, a tub of hot water and salts for his tired feet, and, more than anything, needing somebody—anybody—who was more concerned about where he would spend eternity than where he would spend Friday's paycheck.

Or that he resisted the urge to fry the two-bit, self-appointed hall monitors of holiness who dared to suggest that he was doing the work of the devil.

Not that he kept his cool while the dozen best friends he ever had felt the heat and got out of the kitchen. Or that he gave no command to the angels who begged, "Just give the nod, Lord. One word and these demons will be deviled eggs."

Not that he refused to defend himself when blamed for every sin of every sex worker and sailor since Adam. Or that he stood silent as a million guilty verdicts echoed in the tribunal of heaven and the giver of light was left in the chill of a sinner's night.

Not even that after three days in a dark hole, he stepped into the Easter sunrise with a smile and a swagger and a question for lowly Lucifer—"Is that your best punch?"

That was cool, incredibly cool.

But want to know the coolest thing about the One who gave up the crown of heaven for a crown of thorns?

He did it for you. Just for you.

Chapter 4

Jesus Gets You

I am watching a family of black-tailed squirrels. I should be working on a Christmas message but can't focus. They seem set on entertaining me. They scamper amid the roots of the tree north of my office. We've been neighbors for three years now. They watch me peck at the keyboard. I watch them store their nuts and climb the trunk. We're mutually amused. I could watch them all day. Sometimes I do.

But I've never considered becoming one of them. The squirrel world holds no appeal to me. Who wants to sleep next to a hairy rodent with beady eyes? (No comments from you, Denalyn.) Give up the Rocky Mountains, bass fishing, weddings, and laughter for a hole in the ground and a diet of dirty nuts? Count me out.

But count Jesus in. What a world he left. Our classiest mansion would be a tree trunk to him. Earth's finest cuisine would be walnuts on heaven's table. And the idea of becoming a squirrel with claws and tiny teeth and a furry tail? It's nothing compared to God's becoming an embryo and entering the womb of Mary.

Nonetheless, he did. The God of the universe was born into the poverty of a peasant and spent his first night in the feed trough of a cow. "The Word became flesh and lived among us" (John 1:14 NRSV). The God of the universe left the glory of heaven and moved into the neighborhood. Our neighborhood! Who could have imagined he would do such a thing?

He loves to be with the ones he loves, so much so that the One who made everything "made himself nothing" (Phil. 2:7 NCV). Christ made himself small. He made himself dependent on lungs, a larynx, and legs. He experienced hunger and thirst. He went through all the normal stages of human development. He was taught to walk, stand, wash his face, and dress himself. His muscles grew stronger; his hair grew longer. His voice cracked when he passed through puberty. He was genuinely human.

When he was "full of joy" (Luke 10:21), his joy was authentic. When he wept for Jerusalem (Luke 19:41), his tears were as real as yours or mine. When he asked, "How long must I put up with you?" (Matt. 17:17 NLT), his frustration was honest. When he cried out from the cross, "My God, my God, why have you forsaken me?" (Matt. 27:46), he needed an answer.

He took "the very nature of a servant" (Phil. 2:7). He became like us so he could serve us! He entered the world not to demand our allegiance but to display his affection.

Jesus may have had pimples. He may have been tone deaf. Perhaps a girl down the street had a crush on him or vice versa. It could be that his knees were bony. One thing's for sure: he was, while completely divine, completely human.

Why? Why did Jesus expose himself to human difficulties? Growing weary in Samaria (John 4:6). Disturbed in Nazareth (Mark 6:6). Angry in the temple (John 2:15). Sleepy in the boat on the Sea of Galilee (Mark 4:38). Sad at the tomb of Lazarus (John 11:35). Hungry in the wilderness (Matt. 4:2).

Why did he endure all these feelings? Because he knew you would feel them too. He knew you would be weary, disturbed, and angry.

He knew you'd be sleepy, grief stricken, and hungry. He knew you'd face pain. If not the pain of the body, the pain of the soul . . . pain too sharp for any drug. He knew you'd face thirst. If not a thirst for water, at least a thirst for truth, and the truth we glean from the image of a thirsty Christ is that he understands. And because he understands, we can go to him.

Wouldn't his lack of understanding keep us from him? Doesn't the lack of understanding keep us from others? Suppose you were discouraged because of your financial state and needed some guidance from a sympathetic friend. Would you go to the son of a zillionaire? (Remember, you're asking for guidance, not a handout.) Would you approach someone who inherited a fortune? Probably not. Why? He would not understand. He's likely never been where you are, so he can't relate to how you feel.

Jesus, however, has and can. He has been where you are and can relate to how you feel. And if his life on earth doesn't convince you, his death on the cross should. He understands what you are going through. Our Lord does not patronize us or scoff at our needs. He responds "generously to all without finding fault" (James 1:5). How can he do this? No one penned it more clearly than the author of Hebrews.

> Jesus understands every weakness of ours, because he was tempted in every way that we are. But he did not sin! So whenever we are in need, we should come bravely before the throne of our merciful God. There we will be treated with undeserved kindness, and we will find help. (Heb. 4:15–16 CEV)

For thirty-three years he felt everything you and I have felt. He felt weak. He grew weary. He was afraid of failure. He was susceptible to wooing women. He got colds, burped, and had body odor. His feelings got hurt. His feet got tired. And his head ached.

To think of Jesus in such a light is . . . Well, it seems almost irreverent, doesn't it? It's not something we like to do; it's uncomfortable. It is much easier to keep the humanity out of the incarnation. Clean the manure from around the manger. Wipe the sweat out of his eyes. Pretend he never snored or blew his nose or hit his thumb with a hammer.

He's easier to handle that way. Something about keeping him divine also keeps him distant, packaged, predictable.

But don't do it. For heaven's sake don't. Let him be as human as he intended to be. Let him into the mire and muck of our world, for only if we let him in, can he pull us out.

Let him in, and listen to him.

"Love your neighbor" (Matt. 22:39 NCV) was spoken by a man whose neighbors tried to kill him.

The challenge to leave family for the gospel (Luke 14:26) was issued by the One who kissed his mother goodbye in the doorway.

"Pray for those who persecute you" (Matt. 5:44) came from the lips that would soon be begging God to forgive his murderers.

"I am with you always" (Matt. 28:20) are the words of a God who in one instant did the impossible to make it all possible for you and me.

God came to earth.

It all happened in a moment. In one moment . . . a most remarkable moment. The Word became flesh.

There will be another. The world will see another instantaneous transformation. In becoming human God made it possible for humans to see God. When Jesus went home, he left the back door open. As a result "in a moment, in the twinkling of an eye, . . . we shall be changed" (1 Cor. 15:52 KJV).

The first moment of transformation went unnoticed by the world. But the second one won't. The next time you use the phrase "just a moment," remember that's all the time it will take to change this world.

PART 2

FRIEND

Cataloged in the file entitled "Maybe this wasn't such a good idea" is an account of the day I nearly fell out of the sky. I was riding in the back of a single-engine plane when, well, let's just say, had I been a Catholic, I would have rubbed the rosaries raw.

The story began when my flight lessons did. That's correct. I decided I wanted to get my pilot's license. It dawned on me one afternoon during a four-hour layover that maybe travel would be simpler if I could handle it myself. I'd heard of people doing it: Orville and Wilbur–types who satisfied the FAA's requirements and set out for their destinations with the ease of a commuter driving to work. No more airport parking garages, no more flight delays, no more serpentine security lines. Sounded good to me.

So I set out to learn to fly. And within twenty or so hours of instruction, I can honestly say I succeeded. I knew how to fly a plane! I could take off. I could turn right and left, ascend, descend, accelerate, decelerate. Just call me Lindbergh. I knew how to fly a plane.

What I didn't know was how to land a plane.

On the day I nearly fell from the sky, I had completed a lesson and employed my instructor, Hank, to fly me to Dallas for a speaking engagement. A good friend was traveling with me, and since I'd spent the morning in the plane, I offered the front seat to him, and I climbed in the back. This left him in the copilot's position and me in the snoozing position. I was well into a good nap when I heard the voice of Hank come over our earphones.

"Guys, I'm about to be sick."

I sat up and leaned forward. Hank was the color of the clouds around us. Tiny beads of sweat were popping out on his forehead. Earlier that day he'd mentioned that his kids were home sick with a virus. I'm no doctor, but I deduced that the virus wasn't limited to Hank's home.

"Say that again, Hank?" I asked.

"I gotta put this plane down. I'm not able to fly."

In the book entitled *Words You Never Want to Hear a Pilot Say*, that phrase deserves its own chapter. Hank set about the task of finding the nearest airport, and I set about the task of searching for rosary beads. As I mentioned earlier, I was in the back seat. Had I been in the front, I might have felt better. I'd never landed a plane, but I had tried. And if Hank passed out, at least I knew how to descend. But I was in the back, absolutely unable to do anything. I couldn't reach the controls. I couldn't radio for help. I couldn't fly the plane. I couldn't even blame anyone. I was utterly, totally, entirely helpless.

Ever been there?

Not in a plane perhaps, but in a courtroom, in a doctor's office, in a jail cell. In a tight place, in a squeeze, in a pickle. With a rock on one side and a hard place on the other, you can't do anything.

It's not that there is little you can do or that you have limited resources to use or restricted options at your disposal. You can do nothing.

Nothing, that is, except turn to Jesus. You may be out of options, but according to the Bible you are never out of hope. Jesus came for the helpless and the hapless. He came as a friend. And he knows how to land this plane called life.

By the way, we landed safely. Hank held control over his stomach long enough to spot a landing strip that sat in the middle of a cotton field and to bring the plane down. I've put my flying lessons on hold. For some reason I'm more interested in hiking boots than airplane wings.

Chapter 5

Life with Joy and Abundance

I have a sketch of Jesus laughing. It hangs on the wall across from my desk.

It's quite a drawing. His head is back. His mouth is open. His eyes are sparkling. He isn't just grinning. He isn't just chuckling. He's roaring. He hasn't heard or seen something like that in quite a while. He's having trouble catching his breath.

It was given to me by an Episcopal priest who carries cigars in his pocket and collects portraits of Jesus smiling. "I give them to anyone who might be inclined to take God too seriously," he explained as he handed me the gift.

He pegged me well.

I'm not one who easily envisions a smiling God. A weeping God, yes. An angry God, okay. A mighty God, you bet. But a chuckling God? It seems too . . . too . . . too unlike what God should do—and be. Which just shows how much I know—or don't know—about God.

What do I think he was doing when he stretched the neck of the giraffe? An exercise in engineering? What do I think he had in mind when he told the ostrich where to put his head? Spelunking? What do I think he was doing when he designed the mating call of an ape? Or the eight legs of the octopus? And what do I envision on his face when he saw Adam's first glance at Eve? A yawn?

Hardly.

As my vision improves and I'm able to read without my stained glasses, I'm seeing that a sense of humor is perhaps the only way God has put up with us for so long.

Is that God with a smile as Moses does a double take at the burning bush that speaks?

Is he smiling again as Jonah lands on the beach, dripping gastric juices and smelling like whale breath?

Is that a twinkle in his eye as he watches the disciples feed thousands with one boy's lunch?

Do you think his face is deadpan as he speaks about the man with a two-by-four in his eye who points out a speck in a friend's eye?

Can you honestly imagine a somber Jesus bouncing children on his knee?

No, I think Jesus smiled. I think he smiled a bit *at* people and a lot *with* people. I think he was the type of guy that people wanted to be near. I think he was the type of guy who was always invited to the party.

Consider, for example, the wedding at Cana. We often talk about this wedding as the place where Jesus turned the water into wine. But why did Jesus go to the wedding in the first place? The answer is found in the second verse of John 2: "Jesus and his followers were also invited to the wedding" (NCV).

When the bride and groom were putting the guest list together, Jesus' name was included. And when Jesus showed up with a half-dozen friends, the invitation wasn't rescinded. Whoever was hosting this party was happy to have Jesus present.

"Be sure to put Jesus' name on the list," he might have said. "He really lightens up a party."

Jesus wasn't invited because he was a celebrity. He wasn't one yet. The invitation wasn't motivated by his miracles. He'd yet to perform any. Why did they invite him?

I suppose they liked him. Big deal? I think so. I think it's significant that common folk in a little town enjoyed being with Jesus. I think it's noteworthy that the Almighty didn't act high and mighty. The Holy One wasn't holier-than-thou. The One who knew it all wasn't a know-it-all. The One who made the stars didn't keep his head in them. The One who owns all the stuff on earth never strutted it.

Never. He could have. Oh, how he could have!

He could have been a name dropper: *Did I ever tell you about the time Moses and I went up on the mountain?*

He could have been a show-off: *Hey, want me to beam you into the twentieth century?*

He could have been a smart aleck: *I know what you're thinking. Want me to prove it?*

He could have been highbrow and uppity: *I've got some property on Jupiter . . .*

Jesus could have been all of these, but he wasn't.

His purpose was not to show off but to show up. He went to great pains to be as human as the guy down the street. He didn't need to study, but he still went to the synagogue. He had no need for income, but he still worked in the workshop. He had known the fellowship of angels and had heard the harps of heaven, yet he still went to parties thrown by tax collectors. And upon his shoulders rested the challenge of redeeming creation, but he still took time to walk for miles to go to a wedding in Cana.

As a result people liked him. Oh, there were those who chaffed at his claims. They called him a blasphemer, but they never called him a braggart. They accused him of heresy but never arrogance. He was branded as a radical but never called unapproachable.

There is no hint that he ever used his heavenly status for personal gain. Ever. You don't get the impression that his neighbors grew sick of his haughtiness and asked, "Well, who do you think made you God?"

His faith made him likable, not detestable. Jesus was accused of much, but of being a grump, sourpuss, or self-centered jerk? No. People didn't groan when he appeared. They didn't duck for cover when he entered the room.

He called them by name.

He listened to their stories.

He answered their questions.

He visited their sick relatives and helped their sick friends.

He fished with fishermen and ate lunch with the little guy and spoke words of resounding affirmation. He went to enough parties that he was criticized for hanging out with rowdy people and questionable crowds.

People were drawn to Jesus. He was always on the guest list. Thousands came to hear him. Hundreds chose to follow him. They shut down their businesses and walked away from careers to be with him. His purpose statement read: "I came to give life with joy and abundance" (John 10:10 THE VOICE). Jesus was happy and wants us to be the same.

When the angels announced the arrival of the Messiah, they proclaimed "good news of a great joy" (Luke 2:10 RSV), not "bad news of a great duty."

Would people say the same of us? Where did we get the notion that a good Christian is a solemn Christian? Who started the rumor that the sign of a disciple is a long face? How did we create this idea that the truly gifted are the heavyhearted?

May I state an opinion that could raise an eyebrow? May I tell you why I think Jesus went to that wedding in Cana? I think he went to the wedding to—now hold on, hear me out—I think Jesus went to the wedding to have fun.

Think about it. It had been a tough season. This wedding occurred after he had just spent forty days in the desert. No food or water. A standoff with the devil. A week breaking in some greenhorn Galileans. A job change. He had left home. It hadn't been easy. A break would be welcome. Good meal with some good wine and some good friends . . . Well, it sounded pretty nice.

So off they went.

His purpose wasn't to turn the water into wine. That was a favor for his friends.

His purpose wasn't to show his power. The wedding host didn't even know what Jesus did.

His purpose wasn't to preach. There is no record of a sermon.

This leaves only one reason. Fun. Jesus went to the wedding because he liked the people, he liked the food, and, heaven forbid, he may have even wanted to swirl the bride around the dance floor a time or two. (After all, he's planning a big wedding himself. Maybe he wanted the practice?)

So forgive me, Deacon Drydust and Sister Somberheart. I'm sorry to rain on your dirge, but Jesus was a likable fellow. And his disciples should be the same. I'm not talking debauchery, drunkenness, and adultery. I'm not endorsing compromise, coarseness, or obscenity. I am simply crusading for the freedom to enjoy a good joke, enliven a dull party, and appreciate a fun evening.

Maybe these thoughts catch you by surprise. They do me. It's been a while since I pegged Jesus as a party lover. But he was. His foes accused him of eating too much, drinking too much, and hanging out with the wrong people! I must confess: it's been a while since I've been accused of having too much fun. How about you?

Remember that sketch of Jesus hanging in my office? What sort of portrait of Jesus hangs on the walls of your mind? Is he sad, somber, angry? Are his lips pursed? Is he judging you? If so, visualize the laughing Christ on my wall. I've needed the reminder more times than I can say. Jesus laughed. He had fun. He was always invited to the party, because people wanted to be near him.

They didn't fear his judgment. They knew he wouldn't try to shut things down.

Who could be relied on to be the life of the party more than the One who came to give life with joy and abundance?

Chapter 6

Grace and Truth

Combine the greed of an embezzling executive with the presumption of a hokey television evangelist. Throw in the audacity of an ambulance-chasing lawyer and the cowardice of a drive-by sniper. Stir in a pinch of a pimp's morality, and finish it off with the drug peddler's code of ethics, and what do you have?

A first-century tax collector.

According to the Jews these guys ranked barely above plankton on the food chain. Caesar permitted these Jewish citizens to tax almost anything—your boat, the fish you caught, your house, your crops. Tax collectors made a handsome income by giving Rome its due and pocketing the rest.

Matthew was a public tax collector. Private tax collectors hired other people to do the dirty work. Public publicans, like Matthew, just pulled their stretch limos into the poor side of town and set up shop. As crooked as corkscrews.

His given name, Levi, was a priestly name (Mark 2:14; Luke 5:27–28). Did his parents aspire for him to enter the priesthood? If so, he was a flop in the family circle.

You can bet he was shunned. The neighborhood cookouts? Never invited. High school reunions? Somehow his name was left off the list. The guy was avoided like group A streptococcus. Everybody kept his distance from Matthew.

Everyone except Jesus. "'Follow me and be my disciple,' Jesus said to him. So Matthew got up and followed him" (Matt. 9:9 NLT).

Matthew must have been ripe. Jesus hardly had to tug. In short order Matthew's shady friends and Jesus' green followers were swapping e-mail addresses. "Then Levi gave a big dinner for Jesus at his house. Many tax collectors and other people were eating there, too" (Luke 5:29 NCV).

What do you suppose led up to that party? Let's try to imagine. I can see Matthew going back to his office and packing up. He removes the Hustler of the Year Award from the wall and boxes up the Shady Business School certificate. His coworkers start asking questions.

"What's up, Matt? Headed on a cruise?"

"Hey, Matthew, the missus kick you out?"

Matthew doesn't know what to say. He mumbles something about a job change. But as he reaches the door, he pauses. Holding his box full of office supplies, he looks back. They're giving him hangdog looks—kind of sad, puzzled.

He feels a lump in his throat. Oh, these guys aren't much. Parents warn their kids about this sort. Salty language. Mardi Gras morals. They keep the phone number of the bookie on speed dial. The bouncer at the gentlemen's club sends them birthday cards. But a friend is a friend. Yet what can he do? Invite them to meet Jesus? Yeah, right. They like preachers the way sheep like butchers. Tell them to tune in to the religious channel on TV? Then they'd think cotton-candy hair is a requirement for following Christ. What if he sneaked little Torah tracts into their desks? Nah, they don't read.

So, not knowing what else to do, he shrugs his shoulders and gives them a nod. "These stupid allergies," he says, rubbing the mist from one eye.

Later that day the same thing happens. He goes to the bar to settle up his account. The decor is blue-collar chic: a seedy, smoky place with a Budweiser chandelier over the pool table and a jukebox in the corner. Not the country club, but for Matthew it's his home on the way home. And when he tells the owner he's moving on, the bartender responds, "Whoa, Matt. What's comin' down?"

Matthew mumbles an excuse about a transfer but leaves with an empty feeling in his gut.

Later on he meets up with Jesus at a diner and shares his problem. "It's my buddies—you know, the guys at the office. And the fellows at the bar."

"What about them?" Jesus asks.

"Well, we kinda run together, you know. I'm gonna miss 'em. Take Josh for instance—as slick as a can of Quaker State, but he visits orphans on Sunday. And Bruno at the gym? Can crunch you like a roach, but I've never had a better friend. He's posted bail for me three times."

Jesus motions for him to go on. "What's the problem?"

"Well, I'm gonna miss those guys. I mean, I've got nothing against Peter and James and John, Jesus . . . but they're Sunday morning, and I'm Saturday night. I've got my own circle, ya know?"

Jesus starts to smile and shake his head. "Matthew, Matthew, you think I came to quarantine you? Following me doesn't mean forgetting your friends. Just the opposite. I want to meet them."

"Are you serious?"

"Is the high priest a Jew?"

"But, Jesus, these guys . . . Half of them are on parole. Josh hasn't worn socks since his bar mitzvah . . ."

"I'm not talking about a religious service, Matthew. Let me ask you, What do you like to do? Bowl? Play Monopoly? How's your golf game?"

Matthew's eyes brighten. "You ought to see me cook. I get on steaks like a whale on Jonah."

"Perfect." Jesus smiles. "Then throw a little going-away party. A hang-up-the-clipboard bash. Get the gang together."

Matthew's all over it. Calling his housekeeper and his secretary and firing up the grill. "Get the word out, Thelma. Drinks and dinner at my house tonight. Tell the guys to come and bring a date."

And so Jesus ends up at Matthew's house, a classy split-level with a view of the Sea of Galilee. Parked out front is everything from BMWs to Harleys to limos. And the crowd inside tells you this is anything but a clergy conference.

Earrings on the guys and tattoos on the girls. Moussified hair.

Music that rumbles teeth roots. And buzzing around in the middle of the group is Matthew, making more connections than an electrician. He hooks up Peter with the tax collector bass club and Martha with the kitchen staff. Simon the Zealot meets a high school debate partner. And Jesus? Beaming. What could be better? Sinners and saints in the same room, and no one's trying to determine who is which. But an hour or so into the evening the door opens, and an icy breeze blows in. "The Pharisees and the men who taught the law for the Pharisees began to complain to Jesus' followers, 'Why do you eat and drink with tax collectors and sinners?'" (Luke 5:30 NCV).

Enter the religious police and their thin-lipped piety. Big black books under their arms. Cheerful as Siberian prison guards. Clerical collars so tight that veins bulge. They like to grill too. But not steaks.

Matthew is the first to feel the heat. "Some religious fellow you are," one says, practically pulling an eyebrow muscle. "Look at the people you hang out with."

Matthew doesn't know whether to get mad or get out. Before he has time to choose, Jesus intervenes, explaining that Matthew is right where he needs to be. "Healthy people don't need a doctor— sick people do. I have come to call not those who think they are righteous, but those who know they are sinners and need to repent" (vv. 31–32 NLT).

Jesus peppered the sentence with irony. Pharisees considered themselves spiritually "healthy" and "righteous." In actuality they were unhealthy and self-righteous. But since they did not think they were sick, they saw no need for Jesus.

Matthew and the gang, on the other hand, made room for Jesus. As a result Jesus made room for them.

Do we?

One of the most difficult relationship questions is "What do we do with Levi?"

Your Levi is the person with whom you fundamentally disagree. You follow different value systems. You embrace different philosophies. You adhere to different codes of behavior, dress, and faith.

How does God want us to respond to the Levis of the world? Ignore them? Share a meal with them? Leave the room when they enter? Ask them to leave so we can stay? Discuss our differences? Dismiss our differences? Argue?

I wonder if the best answer might be found in the short admonition to "accept one another, then, just as Christ accepted you, in order to bring praise to God" (Rom. 15:7).

This passage summarizes a thirty-verse appeal to the Roman church for unity (Rom. 14:1–15:7). Paul begins and ends the treatise with the same verb: *accept*. This verb, *paralambano*, means more than tolerate or coexist. It means to welcome into one's fellowship and heart. The word implies the warmth and kindness of genuine love.

Paul employed the verb when he urged Philemon to welcome the slave Onesimus the same way he would welcome Paul himself (Philem. v. 17). Luke selected it to describe the hospitality of the Maltese to those who were shipwrecked (Acts 28:2). And, most notably, Jesus used it to describe the manner in which he receives us (John 14:3).

How does he receive us? I know how he treated me.

I was a twenty-year-old troublemaker on a downhill path. Though I'd made a commitment to Christ a decade earlier, you wouldn't have known it by the way I lived. I'd spent five years claiming to be God's son on Sunday mornings and buddying with the devil on Saturday nights. I was a hypocrite: two-faced, too fast, and self-centered.

I was lost. Lost as Levi.

When I finally grew weary of sitting in pig slop, I got wind of God's grace. I came to Jesus, and he welcomed me back. Please note: Jesus didn't accept my behavior. He didn't endorse my brawling and troublemaking. He wasn't keen on my self-indulgence and prejudice. My proclivity to boast, manipulate, and exaggerate? The chauvinistic attitude? All that had to go. Jesus didn't gloss over the self-centered Max I had manufactured. He didn't accept my sinful behavior.

But he accepted me, his wayward child. He accepted what he could do with me. He didn't tell me to clean up and then come back. He said, "Come back, and I'll clean you up." He was "full of grace and truth" (John 1:14). Not just grace, but truth; not just truth, but grace.

Grace and truth.

Grace told the adulterous woman, "I do not condemn you" (John 8:11 NASB).

Truth told her, "Go and sin no more" (v. 11 NKJV).

Grace invited a swindler named Zacchaeus to lunch.

Truth prompted him to sell half of his belongings and give to the poor (Luke 19:1–8).

Grace washed the feet of the disciples.

Truth told them, "Do as I have done to you" (John 13:15 NKJV).

Grace invited Peter to climb out of the boat and walk on the sea.

Truth upbraided his lack of faith (Matt. 14:29–31).

Grace invited the woman at the well to drink everlasting water.

Truth tactfully reminded her that she had gone through five husbands and was shacking up with a boyfriend (John 4:18).

Jesus was gracious enough to meet Nicodemus at night.

He was truthful enough to tell him, "Unless one is born of water and the Spirit, he cannot enter the kingdom of God" (John 3:5 NKJV).

Jesus shared truth, but graciously.

Jesus offered grace, but truthfully. Grace and truth. Acceptance seeks to offer both.

Jesus found a way to accept the Matthews and the Maxes of the world. Here is hoping he will do the same through you and me.

Chapter 7

Whoever

"For God so loved the world that he gave his one and only Son, that whoever believes in him shall not perish but have eternal life" (John 3:16).

Whoever unfurls 3:16 as a banner for the ages. *Whoever* unrolls the welcome mat of heaven to humanity. *Whoever* invites the world to God.

Jesus could have so easily narrowed the scope, changing *whoever* into *whatever*. "Whatever Jew believes" or "Whatever woman follows me." But he used no qualifier. The pronoun is wonderfully indefinite. After all, who isn't a *whoever*?

The word sledgehammers racial fences and dynamites social classes. It bypasses gender borders and surpasses ancient traditions.

Whoever makes it clear: God exports his grace worldwide. For those who attempt to restrict it, Jesus has a word: *whoever.*

> *Whoever* acknowledges me before others, I will also acknowledge before my Father in heaven. (Matt. 10:32)

> *Whoever* finds his life will lose it, and whoever loses his life for my sake will find it. (Matt. 10:39 ESV)

> *Whoever* does God's will is my brother and sister and mother. (Mark 3:35)

> *Whoever* believes and is baptized will be saved, but whoever does not believe will be condemned. (Mark 16:16)

> *Whoever* believes in the Son has eternal life, but whoever rejects the Son will not see life, for God's wrath remains on them. (John 3:36)

> *Whoever* drinks the water I give them will never thirst. (John 4:14)

> *Whoever* comes to me I will never drive away. (John 6:37)

> *Whoever* lives by believing in me will never die. (John 11:26)

> *Whoever* desires, let him take the water of life freely. (Rev. 22:17 NKJV, emphasis added in this and the previous verses)

Titus 2:11 assures us that "God's grace that can save everyone has come" (NCV). Paul contended that Jesus Christ "sacrificed himself to win freedom for all mankind" (1 Tim. 2:6 NEB). Peter affirmed that "it is not his [God's] will for any to be lost, but for all to come to repentance" (2 Peter 3:9 NEB). God's gospel has a "whoever" policy.

We humans aren't prone to this "whoever" policy. We're prone to pecking orders. We love the high horse. The boy over the girl or the girl over the boy. The affluent over the destitute. The educated over the dropout. The old-timer over the newcomer. The Jew over the Gentile.

An impassable gulf yawned between Jews and Gentiles in the days of the early church. A Jew could not drink milk drawn by Gentiles or eat their food. Jews could not aid a Gentile mother in her hour of need. Jewish physicians could not attend to non-Jewish patients.[1] No Jew would have anything to do with a Gentile. They were unclean.

Unless that Jew, of course, was Jesus. Suspicions of a new order began to surface because of his curious conversation with the Canaanite woman. Her daughter was dying, and her prayer was urgent. Yet her ancestry was Gentile. "I was sent only to help God's lost sheep—the people of Israel," Jesus told her. "That's true, Lord," she replied, "but even dogs are allowed to eat the scraps that fall beneath their masters' table" (Matt. 15:24, 27 NLT).

Jesus healed the woman's daughter and made his position clear. He was more concerned about bringing everyone in than shutting certain people out.

Not only was Jesus always invited to the party, but also we

are always invited to his. From the person voted most popular to the one voted . . . nothing, because nobody knew she existed. In fact, the latter category is Jesus' specialty. Jesus was a friend to the outcast. He was a friend to the friendless. He hung out with the unpopular, the homeless, the sick.

And the woman everyone was gossiping about. By the time Jesus met her, she was on a first-century version of a downward spiral. Five ex-husbands and half a dozen kids, each looking like a different daddy. Decades of loose living had left her tattooed and tabooed and living with a boyfriend who thought a wedding was a waste of time.

Gossipers wagged their tongues about her. How else can we explain her midday appearance at the water well? Other women filled their buckets at sunrise, but this woman opted for noon, preferring, I suppose, the heat of the sun over the heat of their scorn.

Were it not for the appearance of a Stranger, her story would have been lost in the Samaritan sands. But he entered her life with a promise of endless water and quenched thirst. He wasn't put off by her past. Just the opposite. He offered to make music out of her garbage, and she accepted his offer. We know because of what happened next.

Many Samaritans from the village believed in Jesus because the woman had said, "He told me everything I ever did!" When they came out to see him, they begged him to stay in their village. So he stayed for two days, long enough for many more to hear his message and believe. Then they said to the woman, "Now we believe, not just because of what you told us, but because we have heard him ourselves. Now we know that he is indeed the Savior of the world." (John 4:39–42 NLT)

The woman on the margin became the woman with the message. No one else gave her a chance. Jesus gave her the chance of a lifetime. He came for people like her.

Chapter 8

The Con Artist

If the New Testament has a con artist, this is the man. Zacchaeus never met a person he couldn't swindle or saw a dollar he couldn't hustle. He was a "chief tax collector" (Luke 19:2 NKJV). First-century tax collectors fleeced anything that walked. The Roman government allowed them to keep all they could take, after Rome got its portion. Zacchaeus took a lot. "He was rich" (v. 2 NKJV). Two-seat-roadster rich. Alligator-shoes rich. Tailored-suit and manicured-nails rich. Filthy rich.

And guilty rich? He wouldn't be the first shyster to feel regrets. And he wouldn't be the first to wonder if Jesus could help him shake them. Maybe that's how he ended up in the tree. When Jesus traveled through Jericho, half the town showed up to take a look.

Zacchaeus was among them. Citizens of Jericho weren't about to let short-in-stature, long-on-enemies Zacchaeus elbow his way to the front of the crowd. He was left hopping up and down behind the wall of people, hoping to get a glimpse.

That's when he spotted the sycamore, shimmied up, and scurried out. He was happy to go out on a limb to get a good look at Christ. He never imagined that Christ would take a good look at him. But Jesus did. "Zacchaeus, come down immediately. I must stay at your house today" (v. 5).

The pint-sized petty thief looked to one side, then the other, in case another Zacchaeus was in the tree. Turns out, Jesus was talking to him. To him! Of all the homes in town, Jesus selected Zack's. Financed with illegal money and avoided by neighbors, yet on that day it was graced by the presence of Jesus.

Zacchaeus was never quite the same. "Look, Lord! Here and now I give half of my possessions to the poor, and if I have cheated anybody out of anything, I will pay back four times the amount" (v. 8).

Grace walked in the front door, and selfishness scampered out the back. It changed his heart.

Is grace changing yours?

If there was anything Jesus wanted everyone to understand, it was this: a person is worth something simply because he or she is a person. That is why he treated the outcasts—Samaritans, adulteresses, tax collectors—the way he did, until his very last breath. Remember the crook on the cross beside him?

If anyone was ever worthless, this one was. If any man ever deserved dying, this man probably did. If any fellow was ever a loser, this fellow was at the top of the list.

Perhaps that is why Jesus chose him to show us what he thinks of the human race.

Maybe this criminal had heard the Messiah speak. Maybe he had seen him love the lowly. Maybe he had watched him dine with the punks, pickpockets, and potty mouths on the streets. Or maybe not. Maybe the only thing he knew about this Messiah was what he now saw: a beaten, slashed, nail-suspended preacher. His face crimson with blood, his bones peeking through torn flesh, his lungs gasping for air.

Something, though, told him he had never been in better company. And somehow he realized that even though all he had was prayer, he had finally met the One to whom he should pray.

"Any chance that you could put in a good word for me?" (Loose translation.)

"Consider it done."

Now why did Jesus do that? What in the world did he have to gain by promising this desperado a place of honor at the banquet table? What in the world could this chiseling quisling ever offer in return? I mean, the Samaritan woman I can understand. She could go back and tell the tale. And Zacchaeus had some money that he could give. But this guy? What was he going to do? Nothing!

That's the point. Listen closely. Jesus' love does not depend on what we do for him. Not at all. In the eyes of the King, you have value simply because you are. You don't have to look nice or perform well. Your value is inborn.

Period.

Think about that for just a minute. You are valuable just because you exist. Not because of what you do or what you have done, but simply because you are. Remember that. Remember that the next time you are left bobbing in the wake of someone's steamboat ambition. Remember that the next time some trickster tries to hang a bargain basement price tag on your self-worth. The next time someone tries to pass you off as a cheap buy, just think about the way Jesus honors you . . . and smile.

I do. I smile because I know I don't deserve love like that. None of us does. When you get right down to it, any contribution that any of us makes is pretty puny. All of us—even the purest of us—deserve heaven about as much as that crook did. All of us are signing on Jesus' credit card, not ours.

And it also makes me smile to think there is a grinning ex-con walking the golden streets who knows more about grace than a thousand theologians. No one else would have given him a prayer. But in the end that is all he had. And in the end that is all it took.

PART 3

TEACHER

Some years ago Denalyn and I went on a tour of the Eiffel Tower in Paris. The tower was built between 1887 and 1889 and acted as the entrance arch for the Exposition Universelle in 1889, which marked the centennial of the French Revolution. The tower was supposed to stand for only twenty years, but it became a valuable communication tool and has remained as an unmistakable element of the Paris skyline (especially as buildings in the city cannot surpass seven stories). During the German occupation of Paris in World War II, the lift cables were cut, forcing German soldiers to climb the stairs to the top to hoist the swastika. Within hours of the liberation of Paris, the lifts were back in working order.

It is a fascinating iconic structure, and Denalyn and I joined the throng to explore it. Some tourists wore headphones that provided a self-paced tour. Others followed guides and listened at different junctures. Others did not have headphones and did not have a tour guide. They mistakenly assumed they could answer all their questions on their own. That was me. I soon regretted not having the assistance of a headset or tour guide. I had more questions than I had answers. How long did it take to build? Who had the idea to build it? Why this location? Has the building ever been struck by lightning?

Denalyn didn't know. I didn't know. But the guides knew. So I'll confess. I eavesdropped. I loitered on the outskirts of a group and inclined my ear to pick up bits and pieces of the spiel. I learned about the construction time. I learned about the height. What I did not hear was this invitation: "Would any of you like to get to know the designer?" or "Could I interest anyone in a relationship with the architect?" or "The man behind this structure is interested in telling you more in person. Any volunteers?"

Such offers were never made. Why? The designer is dead, for one thing. He no longer inhabits the earth. But even if Gustave Eiffel were still alive, what are the odds that he would make himself available to me? To receive inquiries? To personally entertain questions? No, we cannot know the designer of the Eiffel Tower.

But we can know the designer of the Grand Canyon, the human eye, and the Milky Way galaxy. The architect of the best-known structure in Paris is dead, buried, and unavailable. But the One who furrowed the Hudson Canyon in the seabed of the Atlantic Ocean is not. The creator of the French monument can no longer speak, but the creator of Mount Everest is alive and well. And he invites us to know him.

We cannot emphasize this enough. God wants us to know him!

"Let not the wise boast in their wisdom, nor the mighty in their strength, nor the rich in their wealth. Whoever boasts must boast in this: that he understands and knows Me" (Jer. 9:23–24 THE VOICE).

It is impossible to know the meaning of life if we do not know the Maker of life. And the Maker of life is willing to be our teacher. Jesus came as our guide. He reveals wisdom and truth. We can know, not just facts about God, but his heart, his joy, his passion, his plan, and his sorrows. We are not left alone with our wanderings and wonderings. We have a teacher. His name is Jesus.

Chapter 9

He Stooped for Her

The voices yanked her out of bed.

"Get up, you harlot."

"What kind of woman do you think you are?"

Priests slammed open the bedroom door, threw back the window curtains, and pulled off the covers. Before she felt the warmth of the morning sun, she felt the heat of their scorn.

"Shame on you."

"Pathetic."

"Disgusting."

She scarcely had time to cover her body before they marched her through the narrow streets. Dogs yelped. Roosters ran. Women leaned out their windows. Mothers snatched children off the path.

Merchants peered out the doors of their shops. Jerusalem became a jury and rendered its verdict with glares and crossed arms.

And as if the bedroom raid and parade of shame were inadequate, the men thrust her into the middle of a morning Bible class.

At dawn he appeared again in the temple courts, where all the people gathered around him, and he sat down to teach them. The teachers of the law and the Pharisees brought in a woman caught in adultery. They made her stand before the group and said to Jesus, "Teacher, this woman was caught in the act of adultery. In the Law Moses commanded us to stone such women. Now what do you say?" (John 8:2–5).

Stunned students stood on one side of her. Pious plaintiffs on the other. They had their questions and convictions; she had her dangling negligee and smeared lipstick. Caught in the act. In the moment. In the arms. In the passion. Caught by the Jerusalem Council on Decency and Conduct. "In the Law Moses commanded us to stone such women. Now what do you say?"

The woman had no exit. Deny the accusation? She had been caught. Plead for mercy? From whom? From God? His spokesmen were squeezing stones and snarling their lips. No one would speak for her.

But someone would stoop for her.

"Jesus stooped down and wrote in the dust" (v. 6 NLT). We would expect him to stand up, step forward, or even ascend a stair and speak. But instead he leaned over. He descended lower than anyone else—beneath the priests, the people, even lower than the woman, perhaps? The accusers looked down on her. To see Jesus, they had to look down even farther.

He's prone to stoop. He stooped to wash feet, to embrace children. Stooped to pull Peter out of the sea, to pray in the garden. He stooped before the Roman whipping post. Stooped to carry the cross. Grace is a God who stoops. Here he stooped to write in the sand.

Remember the first occasion his fingers touched dirt? He scooped soil and formed Adam. As he touched the sun-baked soil beside the woman, Jesus may have been reliving the creation moment, reminding himself from whence we came. Earthly humans are prone to do earthy things. Maybe Jesus wrote in the soil for his own benefit.

Or for hers? To divert gaping eyes from the scantily clad, just-caught woman in the center of the circle?

The posse grew impatient with the silent, stooping Jesus. "They kept demanding an answer, so he stood up" (v. 7 NLT).

He lifted himself erect until his shoulders were straight and his head was high. He stood, not to preach, for his words would be few. Not for long, for he would soon stoop again. Not to instruct his followers; he didn't address them. He stood on behalf of the woman. He placed himself between her and the lynch mob and said, "'All right, but let the one who has never sinned throw the first stone!' Then he stooped down again and wrote in the dust" (vv. 7–8 NLT).

Name callers shut their mouths. Rocks fell to the ground. Jesus resumed his scribbling. "When the accusers heard this, they slipped away one by one, beginning with the oldest, until only Jesus was left in the middle of the crowd with the woman" (v. 9 NLT).

Jesus wasn't finished. He stood one final time and asked the woman, "Where are your accusers?" (v. 10 NLT).

My, my, my. What a question—not just for her but for us. Voices of condemnation awaken us as well.

"You aren't good enough."

"You'll never improve."

"You failed—again."

The voices in our world.

And the voices in our heads! Who is this morality patrolman who issues a citation at every stumble? Who reminds us of every mistake? Does he ever shut up?

No. Because Satan never shuts up. The apostle John called him the accuser:

This great dragon—the ancient serpent called the devil, or Satan, the one deceiving the whole world—was thrown down to the earth with all his angels.

Then I heard a loud voice shouting across the heavens,

". . . For the accuser of our brothers and sisters
    has been thrown down to earth—
the one who accuses them
    before our God day and night." (Rev. 12:9–10 NLT)

Hour after hour, day after day. Relentless, tireless. The accuser makes a career out of accusing. Unlike the conviction of the Holy Spirit, Satan's condemnation brings no repentance or resolve, just regret. He has one aim: "to steal, and to kill, and to destroy" (John 10:10 NKJV).

Steal your peace, kill your dreams, and destroy your future. He has deputized a horde of silver-tongued demons to help him. He enlists people to peddle his poison. Friends dredge up your past. Preachers proclaim all guilt and no grace. And parents, oh, your parents. They own a travel agency that specializes in guilt trips. They distribute it twenty-four hours a day. Long into adulthood you still hear their voices: "Why can't you grow up?" "When are you going to make me proud?"

Condemnation—the preferred commodity of Satan. He will repeat the adulterous woman scenario as often as you permit him to do so, marching you through the city streets and dragging your name through the mud. He pushes you into the center of the crowd and megaphones your sin: "This person was caught in the act of immorality . . . stupidity . . . dishonesty . . . irresponsibility."

But he will not have the last word. Jesus has acted on your behalf.

He stooped. Low enough to sleep in a manger, work in a carpentry shop, sleep in a fishing boat. Low enough to rub shoulders with crooks and lepers. Low enough to be spat upon, slapped, nailed, and speared. Low. Low enough to be buried.

And then he stood. Up from the slab of death. Upright in Joseph's tomb and right in Satan's face. Tall. High. You're invited to the party, all right, the one that will last for eternity. He stood up for the woman and silenced her accusers, and he does the same for you. He stands up . . .

"Where are your accusers? Didn't even one of them condemn you?"

"No, Lord," she said.

And Jesus said, "Neither do I. Go and sin no more." (John 8:10–11 NLT)

Within a few moments the courtyard was empty. Jesus, the woman, her critics—they all left. But let's linger. Look at the rocks on the ground, abandoned and unused. And look at the scribbling in the sand. It's the only sermon Jesus ever wrote. Even though we don't know the words, I'm wondering if they read like this:

Grace happens here.

Chapter 10

One Who Had Authority

Christ: the One and Only Ruler . . . claims to be the One and Only Revealer. "No one truly knows the Son except the Father, and no one truly knows the Father except the Son" (Matt. 11:27 NLT).

Jesus enjoys an intimacy with God, a mutuality shared only in the Trinity.

Married couples know something of this. They finish each other's sentences, anticipate each other's actions. Some even begin to look like each other (a possibility that deeply troubles my wife).

Denalyn and I are closing in on four decades as a married couple. We no longer converse; we communicate in code. She walks into the kitchen while I'm making a sandwich.

"Denalyn?" I ask.

"No, I don't want one."

I'll open the fridge and stare for a few moments. "Denalyn?"

She'll look at my sandwich preparations and answer, "Mayo on the top shelf. Pickles in the door."

She knows what I'll say before I say it. Consequently, she can speak on my behalf with the highest credibility. If she says, "Max would prefer a different color" or "Max would approve this idea," listen to her. She knows what she's talking about. She qualifies as my proxy like no one else.

How much more does Jesus qualify as God's! Jesus "who exists at the very heart of the Father, has made him plain as day" (John 1:18 THE MESSAGE).

When Jesus says, "In My Father's house are many mansions" (John 14:2 NKJV), count on it. He knows. He has walked in them.

When he says, "You are worth more than many sparrows" (Matt. 10:31), trust him. Jesus knows. He knows the value of every creature.

When Christ declares, "Your Father knows what you need before you ask him" (Matt. 6:8 NABRE), believe it. After all, "He was in the beginning with God" (John 1:2 NABRE).

Jesus claims to be, not a top theologian, an accomplished theologian, or even the Supreme Theologian, but rather the Only Theologian. "No one truly knows the Father except the Son." He does not say, "No one truly knows the Father like the Son" or "in the fashion of the Son." But rather, "No one truly knows the Father except the Son."

Heaven's door has one key, and Jesus holds it. Think of it this way. You're a fifth grader studying astronomy. The day you read about the first mission to the moon you and your classmates pepper the teacher with space-travel questions.

"What does moondust feel like?"

"Can you swallow when there's no gravity?"

"What about going to the bathroom?"

The teacher does the best she can but prefaces most replies with "I would guess . . ." or "I think . . ." or "Perhaps . . ."

How could she know? She's never been there. But the next day she brings a guest who has. Buzz Aldrin enters the room. Yes, the astronaut who left footprints on the surface of the moon.

"Now ask your questions," the teacher invites. And Aldrin answers each with certainty. He knows the moon; he's walked on it. No speculation or hesitation. He speaks with conviction.

So did Jesus. "He was teaching them as one who had authority" (Matt. 7:29 ESV). Jesus knows the dimensions of God's throne room, the fragrance of its incense, the favorite songs of the unceasing choir. He has a unique, one-of-a-kind, unrivaled knowledge of God and wants to share his knowledge with you. "No one truly knows the Father except the Son and those to whom the Son chooses to reveal him" (Matt. 11:27 NLT).

Jesus doesn't boast about his knowledge; he shares it. He doesn't gloat; he gives. He doesn't revel; he reveals. He reveals to us the secrets of eternity.

And he shares them, not just with the top brass or purebred, but with the hungry and needy. In the very next line Jesus invites: "Come to me, all of you who are weary and carry heavy burdens, and I will give you rest. Take my yoke upon you. Let me teach you, because I am humble and gentle at heart, and you will find rest for your souls" (vv. 28–29 NLT).

Do yourself a favor. Find the brightest highlighter manufactured and the darkest ink produced. Underscore, underline, and accept his invitation: "Let me teach you . . ."

God is not a God of confusion, and wherever he sees sincere seekers with confused hearts, you can bet your sweet December that he will do whatever it takes to help them see his will.

One of my Boy Scout assignments was to build a kite. One of my blessings as a Boy Scout was a kite-building dad. He built a lot of things: scooters on skates, go-carts. He even built our house. A kite to him was like stick figures to Van Gogh. He could handle them in his sleep.

With wood glue, poles, and newspaper, we fashioned a sky-dancing masterpiece: red, white, and blue and shaped like a box. We launched our creation on the back of a March wind. But after some minutes my kite caught a downdraft and plunged. I tightened the string, raced in reverse, and did all I could to maintain elevation. But it was too late. She Hindenburged earthward.

Envision a redheaded, heartsick twelve-year-old standing over his collapsed kite. That was me. Envision a square-bodied man with ruddy skin and coveralls placing his hand on the boy's shoulder. That was my kite-making dad. He surveyed the heap of sticks and paper and assured me, "It's okay. We can fix this." I believed him. Why not? He spoke with authority.

So does Christ. To all whose lives feel like a crashed kite, he says, "We can fix this. Let me teach you. Let me teach you how to handle your money, long Mondays, and cranky in-laws. Let me teach you why people fight, death comes, and forgiveness counts. But most of all let me teach you why on earth you are on this earth."

Don't we need to learn? We know so much, and yet we know so little. The age of information is the age of confusion. There is much know-how but hardly any know-why. We need answers. Jesus offers them.

But can we trust him? Only one way to know. Seek him out. Lift up your eyes and set your sights on Jesus. No passing glances or occasional glimpses. Enroll in his school. "Let me teach you . . ."

Make him your polestar, your point of reference. Search the crowded streets and shadow-casting roofs until you spot his face, and then set your sights on him.

Chapter 11

The Way Through
the Wilderness

The wilderness of the desert. Parched ground. Sharp rocks. Shifting sand. Burning sun. Thorns that cut. The mirage of an oasis. Wavy horizons ever beyond reach. This is the wilderness of the desert.

The wilderness of the soul. Parched promises. Sharp words. Shifting commitments. Burning anger. Rejections that cut. The mirage of hope. Distant solutions ever beyond reach. This is the wilderness of the soul.

Some of you know the first. All of you know the second. Jesus, however, knew both. With skin still moist with Jordan River water,

———

he turned away from food and friends and entered the country of hyenas, lizards, and vultures. He was "led around by the Spirit in the wilderness for forty days, being tempted by the devil. And He ate nothing during those days, and when they had ended, He became hungry" (Luke 4:1–2 NASB).

The wilderness was not a typical time for Jesus. Normalcy was left at the Jordan and would be rediscovered in Galilee. The wilderness was and is atypical. A dark parenthesis in the story of life. A fierce season of face-to-face encounters with the devil. You needn't journey to Israel to experience the wilderness. A cemetery will do just fine. So will a hospital. Grief can lead you into the desert. So can divorce or debt or depression.

In the Bible the number forty is associated with lengthy battles. Noah faced rain for forty days. Moses faced the desert for forty years. Jesus faced temptation for forty nights. Please note: he didn't face temptation for one day out of forty. Jesus was "in the wilderness for forty days, being tempted by the devil." The battle wasn't limited to three questions. Jesus spent a month and ten days slugging it out with Satan.

The wilderness is a long, lonely winter. Doctor after doctor. Résumé after résumé. Diaper after diaper. Zoloft after Zoloft. Heartache after heartache. The calendar is stuck in February, and you're stuck in South Dakota, and you can't even remember what spring smells like.

One more symptom of the badlands: you think the unthinkable. Jesus did. Wild possibilities crossed his mind. Teaming up with Satan? Opting to be a dictator and not a Savior? Torching Earth and starting over on Pluto? We don't know what he thought. We just know this: Jesus was "tempted by the devil." Satan's words, if but for a moment, gave him pause. He didn't eat the bread, but he stopped long enough in front of the bakery to smell it.

Christ knows the wilderness. More than you might imagine. After all, going there was his idea. Don't blame this episode on Satan. He didn't come to the desert looking for Jesus. Jesus went to the badlands looking for him. "The Spirit led Jesus into the desert *to be tempted* by the devil" (Matt. 4:1 NCV, emphasis mine). Heaven orchestrated this date. How do we explain this?

Does the word *rematch* mean anything to you? For the second time in history, an unfallen mind would face the fallen angel. The Second Adam had come to succeed where the First Adam failed.

Christ dared the devil to climb into the ring. "You've been haunting my children since the beginning. See what you can do with me." And Satan did. For forty days the two went toe to toe. The Son of heaven was tempted but never wavered, was struck but never struck down. He succeeded where Adam failed.

This victory, according to Paul, was a huge victory for us all. "Here it is in a nutshell: Just as one person did it wrong and got us in all this trouble with sin and death, another person did it right and got us out of it" (Rom. 5:18 THE MESSAGE). God gives you Jesus' wilderness grade. Believe that. If you don't, the desert days will give you a one-two punch. The right hook is the struggle. The left jab is the shame for not prevailing against it. Trust his work. And trust his Word. Don't trust your emotions. Don't trust your opinions. Don't even trust your friends. Heed only the voice of God.

Again Jesus is our model. Remember how Satan taunted him? "If you are the Son of God . . ." (Matt. 4:3, 6 NCV). Why would

Satan say this? Because he knew what Christ heard at the baptism: "This is My beloved Son, in whom I am well pleased" (Matt. 3:17 NKJV). "Are you really God's Son?" Satan was asking. Then came the dare—"Prove it! Prove it by doing something":

"Tell these stones to become bread" (Matt. 4:3).

"Throw yourself down" (v. 6).

"If you will bow down and worship me, I will give you all these things" (v. 9 NCV).

What subtle seduction! Satan didn't denounce God; he simply raised doubts about God. Is his work enough? Earthly works—like bread changing or temple jumping—were given equal billing with heavenly works. And he still attempts to shift, ever so gradually, our source of confidence away from God's promise and toward our performance.

Jesus didn't bite the bait. No heavenly sign was requested. He didn't solicit a lightning bolt; he simply quoted the Bible. Three temptations. Three declarations.

"It is written . . ." (v. 4).

"It is also written . . ." (v. 7).

"It is written . . ." (v. 10).

Jesus' survival weapon of choice was Scripture. If the Bible was enough for his wilderness, shouldn't it be enough for ours? Don't miss the point here. Everything you and I need for desert survival is in the Book. We simply need to heed it.

On a trip to the United Kingdom, our family visited a castle. In the center of the garden sat a maze. Row after row of shoulder-high hedges, leading to one dead end after another. Successfully navigate the labyrinth and discover the door to a tall tower in the center of the garden. Were you to look at our family pictures of the trip, you'd see four of our five family members standing on the top of the tower. Hmmm, someone is still on the ground. Guess who? I was stuck in the foliage. I just couldn't figure out which way to go.

Ahhh, but then I heard a voice from above. "Hey, Dad." I looked up, and it was Sara, peering through the turret at the top. "You're going the wrong way," she explained. "Back up and turn right."

Do you think I trusted her? Didn't have to. I could trust my own instincts, consult other confused tourists, sit and pout and wonder why God would let this happen to me. But do you want to know what I did? I listened. Her vantage point was better than mine. She was above the maze. She could see what I couldn't.

Don't you think we should do the same with God? "God is . . . higher than the heavens" (Job 22:12 NLT). "The LORD is high above all nations" (Ps. 113:4 NKJV). Can he not see what we can't? Doesn't he want to get us out and bring us home? Then do what Jesus did. Rely on Scripture. Doubt your doubts before you doubt your beliefs. Jesus told Satan, "Man shall not live on bread alone, but on every word that proceeds out of the mouth of God" (Matt. 4:4 NASB). The verb *proceeds* is literally "pouring out." Its tense suggests that God is constantly and aggressively communicating with the world through his Word. Wow! God is speaking still! Hang in there. Your time in the desert will pass. Jesus' did. "The devil left Him; and behold, angels came and began to minister to Him" (v. 11 NASB).

Till angels come to you:

Trust his Word. You need a voice to lead you out.

Trust his work. You need a friend to take your place.

Thank God you have One who will.

Chapter 12

"I Am the Vine"

Abide in Me, and I in you. As the branch cannot bear fruit of itself unless it abides in the vine, so neither can you unless you abide in Me. I am the vine, you are the branches; he who abides in Me and I in him, he bears much fruit, for apart from Me you can do nothing. If anyone does not abide in Me, he is thrown away as a branch and dries up; and they gather them, and cast them into the fire and they are burned. If you abide in Me, and My words abide in you, ask whatever you wish, and it will be done for you. My Father is glorified by this, that you bear much fruit, and so prove

to be My disciples. Just as the Father has loved Me, I
have also loved you; abide in My love. If you keep My
commandments, you will abide in My love; just as I
have kept My Father's commandments and abide in
His love. (John 15:4–10 NASB)

Jesus' allegory is simple. God is like a vine keeper. He lives and loves to coax the best out of his vines. He pampers, prunes, blesses, and cuts. His aim is singular: "What can I do to prompt produce?" God is a capable orchardist who carefully superintends the vineyard.

And Jesus plays the role of the vine. We nongardeners might confuse the vine and the branch. To see the vine, lower your gaze from the stringy, winding branches to the thick base below. The vine is the root and trunk of the plant. It cables nutrients from the soil to the branches. Jesus makes the stunning claim, "I am the real root of life." If anything good comes into our lives, he is the conduit.

And who are we? We are the branches. We bear fruit: "love, joy, peace, patience, kindness, goodness, faithfulness" (Gal. 5:22 NASB). We meditate on what is "true, and honorable, and right, and pure, and lovely, and admirable . . . excellent and worthy of praise" (Phil. 4:8 NLT). Our gentleness is evident to all. We bask in the "peace of God, which transcends all understanding" (Phil. 4:7).

And as we cling to Christ, God is honored. "My Father is glorified by this, that you bear much fruit, and so prove to be My disciples" (John 15:8 NASB).

The Father tends. Jesus nourishes. We receive, and grapes

appear. Passersby, stunned at the overflowing baskets of love, grace, and peace, can't help but ask, "Who runs this vineyard?" And God is honored. For this reason fruit bearing matters to God.

And it matters to you! You grow weary of unrest. You're ready to be done with sleepless nights. You long for the fruit of the Spirit. But how do you bear this fruit? Try harder? No, hang tighter. Our assignment is not fruitfulness but faithfulness. The secret to fruit bearing and anxiety-free living is less about doing and more about abiding.

Lest we miss this point, Jesus employed the word *abide(s)* ten times in seven verses:

> Abide in Me, and I in you. As the branch cannot bear fruit of itself unless it abides in the vine, so neither can you unless you abide in Me. . . . He who abides in Me and I in him, he bears much fruit . . . If anyone does not abide in Me, he is thrown away as a branch and dries up . . . If you abide in Me, and My words abide in you, ask whatever you wish, and it will be done for you. . . . Abide in My love. . . . Abide in My love; just as I have kept My Father's commandments and abide in His love. (John 15:4–10 NASB)

"Come, live in me!" Jesus invites. "Make my home your home."

Odds are that you know what it means to be at home somewhere.

To be at home is to feel safe. The residence is a place of refuge and security.

To be at home is to be comfortable. You can pad around wearing slippers and a robe.

To be at home is to be familiar. When you enter the door, you needn't consult the blueprint to find the kitchen.

Our aim—our only aim—is to be at home in Christ. He is not a roadside park or hotel room. He is our permanent mailing address. Christ is our home. He is our place of refuge and security. We are comfortable in his presence, free to be our authentic selves. We know our way around in him. We know his heart and his ways.

We rest in him, find our nourishment in him. His roof of grace protects us from storms of guilt. His walls of providence secure us from destructive winds. His fireplace warms us during the lonely winters of life. We linger in the abode of Christ and never leave.

The branch never releases the vine. Ever! Does a branch show up on Sundays for its once-a-week meal? Only at the risk of death. The healthy branch never releases the vine; to do so would interrupt the flow of essential nutrients.

If branches had seminars, the topic would be "Secrets of Vine Grabbing." But branches don't have seminars, because to attend them they would have to release the vine—something they refuse to do. The dominant duty of the branch is to cling to the vine.

The dominant duty of the disciple is the same.

We Christians tend to miss this. We banter about pledges to "change the world," "make a difference for Christ," "lead people to the Lord." Yet these are by-products of the Christ-focused life. Our goal is not to bear fruit. Our goal is to stay attached.

Maybe this image will help. When a father leads his four-year-old son down a crowded street, he takes him by the hand and says, "Hold on to me." He doesn't say, "Memorize the map" or "Take your chances dodging the traffic" or "Let's see if you can find

---

your way home." The good father gives the child one responsibility: "Hold on to my hand."

God does the same with us. Don't load yourself down with lists. Don't enhance your anxiety with the fear of not fulfilling them. Your goal is not to know every detail of the future. Your goal is to hold the hand of the One who does and to never, ever let go.

This was the choice of Kent Brantly.

Brantly was a medical missionary in Liberia, waging a war on the cruelest of viruses, Ebola. The epidemic was killing people by the thousands. As much as any person in the world, Brantly knew the consequences of the disease. He had treated dozens of cases. He knew the symptoms—soaring fever, severe diarrhea, and nausea. He had seen the results of the virus, and for the first time he was feeling the symptoms himself.

His colleagues had drawn blood and begun the tests. But it would be at least three days before they knew the results. On Wednesday evening, July 23, 2014, Dr. Brantly quarantined himself in his house and waited. His wife and family were across the ocean. His coworkers could not enter his residence. He was, quite literally, alone with his thoughts. He opened his Bible and meditated on a passage from the book of Hebrews. Then he wrote in his journal, "The promise of entering his rest still stands, so let us never give up. Let us, therefore, make every effort . . . to enter that rest."[1]

Dr. Brantly considered the phrase "make every effort." He knew he would have to do exactly that. He then turned his attention to another verse from the same chapter in Hebrews: "Let us then approach the throne of grace with confidence, so that we may receive mercy and find grace to help us in our time of need."[2] He copied the scripture into his prayer journal and wrote the words "with confidence" in italics.[3]

He closed his journal and began the wait. The next three days brought unspeakable discomfort. The test results confirmed what they feared: he had contracted Ebola.

Kent's wife, Amber, was in her hometown of Abilene, Texas, when he called her with the diagnosis the following Saturday afternoon. She and their two children were visiting her parents. When her phone rang, she hurried to the bedroom for some privacy. Kent went straight to the point. "The test results came back. It's positive."

She began to cry. They talked for a few moments before Kent said that he was tired and would call again soon.

Now it was Amber's turn to process the news. She and her parents sat on the edge of her bed and wept for several minutes. After some time Amber excused herself and went outside. She walked across a field toward a large mesquite tree and took a seat on a low-hanging branch. She had trouble finding the words to formulate her prayers, so she used the lyrics of hymns she had learned as a young girl.

> There is no shadow of turning with Thee;
> Thou changest not, Thy compassions, they fail not
> As Thou hast been Thou forever wilt be.[4]

The words lifted her spirits, so she began to sing aloud another song she treasured:

> I need Thee every hour, in joy or pain;
> Come quickly and abide, or life is vain.

I need Thee, O I need Thee;
Every hour I need Thee;
O bless me now, my Savior,
I come to Thee.[5]

She later wrote, "I thought my husband was going to die. I was in pain. I was afraid. Through [the singing of] those hymns, though, I was able to connect with God in a meaningful way."[6]

Kent was transported from Africa to Atlanta. His caregivers chose to risk an untested treatment, and little by little his condition improved. Within a few days his strength began to return. The entire world, it seemed, rejoiced when he was able to exit the hospital, cured of Ebola.

We can applaud the Brantlys' victory over another disease, a virus that is every bit as deadly and contagious: the unseen contagion of anxiety. Kent and Amber were prime candidates for panic, yet they reacted with the same resolve that enabled them to battle Ebola. They stayed connected to the vine. They resolved to abide in Christ. Kent opened his Bible. Amber meditated on hymns. They filled their minds with the truth of God.

Jesus taught us to do the same. He tells us, rather bluntly, "Do not worry about your life, what you will eat or what you will drink; nor about your body, what you will put on" (Matt. 6:25 NKJV).

He then gives two commands: "look" and "consider." He tells us to "look at the birds of the air" (Matt. 6:26 NKJV). When we do, we notice how happy they seem to be. They aren't frowning, cranky, or grumpy. They don't appear sleep deprived or lonely.

They sing, whistle, and soar. Yet "they neither sow nor reap nor gather into barns" (v. 26 NKJV). They don't drive tractors or harvest wheat, yet Jesus asks us, Do they appear well cared for?

Next he turns our attention to the flowers of the field. "Consider the lilies" (v. 28 NKJV). By the same token they don't do anything. Even though their life span is short, God dresses them up for red-carpet appearances. Even Solomon, the richest king in history, "was not arrayed like one of these" (v. 29 NKJV).

How do we disarm anxiety? Stockpile our minds with God thoughts. Draw the logical implication: if birds and flowers fall under the category of God's care, won't he care for us as well? Saturate your heart with the goodness of God.

"Set your mind on things above, not on things on the earth" (Col. 3:2 NKJV).

How might you do this?

A friend recently described to me her daily ninety-minute commute.

"Ninety minutes!" I commiserated.

"Don't feel sorry for me." She smiled. "I use the trip to think about God." She went on to describe how she fills the hour and a half with worship and sermons. She listens to entire books of the Bible. She recites prayers. By the time she reaches her place of employment, she is ready for the day. "I turn my commute into my chapel."

Do something similar. Is there a block of time you can claim for God? Perhaps you could turn off the network news and open your Bible. Set the alarm fifteen minutes earlier. Or rather than watch the TV comedian as you fall asleep, listen to an audio version of a Christian book. "If you abide in my word, you are truly my disciples, and you will know the truth, and the truth will set you free" (John 8:31–32 ESV). Free from fear. Free from dread. And, yes, free from anxiety.

PART 4

MIRACLE WORKER

D o you believe in miracles? Do you believe in supernatural interruptions? Do you believe in divine interventions? Are you open to the idea of a God who, at times for his purposes, suspends the natural laws, amends the constitution of the cosmos, bends the arc of history, and creates an unexpected, inexplicable event?

Do you believe in divine miracles?

Not magic. Not sleight of hand. Not hocus-pocus or abracadabra. Do you believe in God-ordained, God-determined, God-directed acts of supernatural good? Not luck. Not fortune. Not balls bouncing in your direction, dice turning up sevens, or stars lining up in your favor.

I'm asking about miracles: eye-opening, jaw-dropping, science-defying, faith-prompting, heart-touching, God-honoring events that no professor, preacher, physicist, or physician can explain.

Do you believe in miracles?

We want to, don't we? The cancer patient does. The unemployed father does. The mom of the wayward child does. The farmer with the drought-stricken crop does. The exhausted physician in the ICU does.

We all do. At some point, some low point, we find ourselves hoping beyond hope for a solution beyond personal resources, longing for a being who is at once unbound and benevolent. A God who is ungoverned by laws of nature, unhindered by weariness, and unlimited in his affection for us.

We desire, do we not, to be released from the rigid train tracks of the predictable, explicable, touchable, measurable, and tangible.

We long to believe in miracles.

But we are hesitant. Careful. Cautious. Charlatans and snake-oil peddlers traffic in this medium. What if we get snookered? What if the promise of miracles is fool's gold on the pathway of disappointment?

Then again, what if the promise of miracles is true? What if the Bible stories have credence? What if the gospel writers weren't kidding when they wrote:

News about [Jesus] spread all over Syria, and people brought to him all who were ill with various diseases, those suffering severe pain, the demon-possessed, those having seizures, and the paralyzed; and he healed them. (Matt. 4:24)

Then [Jesus] arose and rebuked the winds and the sea, and there was a great calm. (Matt. 8:26 NKJV)

Jesus had compassion on them and touched their eyes. Immediately they received their sight and followed him. (Matt. 20:34)

They saw Jesus approaching the boat, walking on the water. (John 6:19)

And as many as touched Him were made well. (Mark 6:56
NKJV)

Verse after verse. Story after story. Event after event. Miracles
so numerous that, were each occasion to be transcribed, "the world
itself could not contain the books that would be written" (John
21:25 NKJV).

The miracles of Jesus were not occasional; they were constant.
They were not marginal to his story; they were essential. They
were not peripheral; they were vital activities upon which the very
identity of Jesus was constructed.

Indeed, one of the most compelling arguments for the verac-
ity of Christ was the *inability* of his adversaries to denounce his
miraculous deeds. Here is an example. A brief fifty days after
the resurrection of Jesus, an emboldened apostle Peter began his
message to an audience of several thousand people in downtown
Jerusalem by saying, "Men of Israel, hear these words: Jesus of
Nazareth, a Man attested by God to you by miracles, wonders, and
signs which God did through Him in your midst, as you yourselves
also know" (Acts 2:22 NKJV).

I like to think that the fisherman-turned-preacher paused after
that statement, letting his words echo off the Jerusalem stone. "As
you yourselves know! . . . know! . . . know! . . ." Did he pause on
purpose, waiting for one person, just one voice, to cry out in dis-
agreement? Did he invite the opposition to react? "Wait a minute.
We *don't* know! We saw nothing! We witnessed no miracles, wonders, or signs!"

But there was no rebuttal. There was no refusal. There were no voices to the contrary. There was, instead, a nodding of heads, an affirming murmur in the crowd. Many of the people had not only seen the miracles; they had been blessed by them.

Can we not assume that some people in the Jerusalem audience were seeing Peter with eyes that were once blind? Stood on legs that were once crippled? Lifted healthy hands that, before Christ, were marred and scarred by leprosy?

No adversary countered the claim of Peter, because no adversary could. The reason that three thousand people responded to Peter's altar call (Acts 2:38–41) was not because his sermon was so eloquent but because Jesus' ministry was so powerful. Case studies were sprinkled throughout the audience.

Would you be open to the idea of a miracle-working Christ? A miracle is a work of God wrought by God for a godly purpose. Miracles are shoulder taps from God, whispers (or sirens) reminding us, *You are not alone. I'm still in charge. My plan will be achieved.*

Miracles remind us that there is more to this life than what meets the eye.

Miracles are "signs . . . [given] that you may believe that Jesus is the Christ, the Son of God, and that believing you may have life in His name" (John 20:30–31 NKJV).

Chapter 13

The Winds and Waves Obey Him

Jesus and the disciples were in a boat crossing the Sea of Galilee. A storm arose suddenly, and what was placid became violent. Monstrous waves rose out of the sea and slapped the boat. Mark described it clearly: "A furious squall came up, and the waves broke over the boat, so that it was nearly swamped" (Mark 4:37).

Imagine yourself in the boat. It's a sturdy vessel but no match for these ten-foot waves. It plunges nose-first into the wall of water. The force of the waves dangerously tips the boat until the bow seems to be pointing straight at the sky, and just when you fear flipping over backward, the vessel pitches forward into the valley of another wave. A dozen sets of hands join yours in clutching the mast. All your shipmates have wet heads and wide eyes. You tune your ear for a calming voice, but all you hear are screams and prayers. All of a sudden it hits you—someone is missing. Where is Jesus? He's not at the mast. He's not grabbing the edge. Where is he? Then you hear something—a noise . . . a displaced sound . . . like someone is snoring. You turn and look, and there curled in the stern of the boat is Jesus, sleeping!

You don't know whether to be amazed or angry, so you're both. How can he sleep at a time like this? Or as the disciples asked, "Teacher, don't you care if we drown?" (Mark 4:38).

If you're a parent of a teenager, you've been asked similar questions. The time you refused to mortgage your house so your daughter could buy the latest-style tennis shoes, she asked, "Don't you care if I look out-of-date?"

When you insisted that your son skip the weekend game and attend his grandparents' golden anniversary, he asked, "Don't you care if I have a social life?"

When you limited the ear piercing to one hole per lobe, the accusation came thinly veiled as a question: "Don't you care if I fit in?"

Do the parents care? Of course they do. It's just that they have a different perspective. What the teenager sees as a storm, mom and dad see as a spring shower. They've been around enough to know these things pass.

So had Jesus. The very storm that made the disciples panic made him drowsy. What put fear in their eyes put him to sleep. The boat was a tomb to the followers and a cradle to Christ. How could he sleep through the storm? Simple, he was in charge of it.

———

The same happens with you and televisions. Ever dozed off with the TV on? Of course you have. But put the same television in the grass hut of a primitive Amazonian Indian who has never seen one, and, believe me, he won't sleep. How could anyone sleep in the presence of a talking box! As far as he knows, those little people behind the glass wall might climb out of the box and come after him. There is no way he's going to sleep. And there is no way he's going to let you sleep either. If you doze off, he'll wake you up. "Don't you care that we're about to be massacred?" Rather than argue with him, what do you do? You just point the remote at the screen and turn it off.

Jesus didn't even need a remote. "He got up, rebuked the wind and said to the waves, 'Quiet! Be still!' Then the wind died down and it was completely calm. He said to his disciples, 'Why are you so afraid? Do you still have no faith?'" (Mark 4:39–40).

Incredible. He didn't chant a mantra or wave a wand. No angels were called; no help was needed. The raging water became a stilled sea, instantly. Immediate calm. Not a ripple. Not a drop. Not a gust. In a moment the sea went from a churning torrent to a peaceful pond. The reaction of the disciples? Read it in verse 41: "They were in absolute awe, staggered. 'Who is this, anyway?' they asked. 'Wind and sea at his beck and call!'" (THE MESSAGE).

They'd never met a man like this. The waves were his subjects, and the winds were his servants. And that was just the beginning of what his sea mates would witness. Before it was over, they would see fish jump into the boat, demons dive into pigs, cripples turn into dancers, and cadavers turn into living, breathing people. "He even gives orders to impure spirits and they obey him," the people proclaimed (Mark 1:27).

Is it any wonder the disciples were willing to die for Jesus? Never had they seen such power; never had they seen such glory. It was like, well, like the whole universe was his kingdom. You wouldn't have needed to explain this verse to them; they knew what it meant: "Thine is the kingdom, and the power, and the glory, for ever" (Matt. 6:13 KJV).

Peter came to experience the miraculous power of Christ first-hand. In another storm, when the boat of the followers threatened to capsize, Jesus came walking on the water toward the disciples. Peter's response was "'Lord, if it is You, command me to come to You on the water.' So He said, 'Come.' And when Peter had come down out of the boat, he walked on the water to go to Jesus" (Matt. 14:28–29 NKJV).

Peter never would have made this request on a calm sea. Had Christ strolled across a lake that was as smooth as mica, Peter would have applauded, but I doubt he would have stepped out of the boat. Storms prompt us to take unprecedented journeys. For a few historic steps and heart-stilling moments, Peter did the impossible. He defied every law of gravity and nature; "he walked on the water to go to Jesus."

My editors wouldn't have tolerated such brevity. They would have flooded the margin with red ink: "Elaborate! How quickly did Peter exit the boat? What were the other disciples doing? What was the expression on his face? Did he step on any fish?"

Matthew had no time for such questions. He moves us quickly to the major message of the event: where to stare in a storm. "But when [Peter] saw that the wind was boisterous, he was afraid; and beginning to sink he cried out, saying, 'Lord, save me!'" (v. 30 NKJV).

A wall of water eclipsed his view. A wind gust snapped the mast with a crack and a slap. A flash of lightning illuminated the lake and the watery Appalachians it had become. Peter shifted his attention away from Jesus and toward the squall, and when he did, he sank like a brick in a pond. Give the storm waters more attention than the Storm Walker, and get ready to do the same.

Whether or not storms come, we cannot choose. But where we stare during a storm, that we can choose. I found a direct example of this truth while sitting in my cardiologist's office. My heart rate had the pace of a NASCAR race and the rhythm of a Morse code message. So I went to a specialist. After reviewing my tests and asking me some questions, the doctor nodded knowingly and asked me to wait for him in his office.

I didn't like being sent to the principal's office as a kid. I don't like being sent to the doctor's office as a patient. But I went in, took a seat, and quickly noticed the doctor's abundant harvest of diplomas. They were everywhere, from everywhere. One degree from the university. Another degree from a residency. The third degree from his wife. (I'm pausing to see if you caught the joke . . .) The more I looked at his accomplishments, the better I felt. *I'm in good hands.*

About the time I leaned back in the chair to relax, his nurse entered with a sheet of paper. "The doctor will be in shortly," she explained. "In the meantime he wants you to acquaint yourself with this information. It summarizes your heart condition." I lowered my gaze from the diplomas to the summary of the disorder. As I read, contrary winds began to blow. Unwelcome words like *atrial fibrillation, arrhythmia, embolic stroke,* and *blood clot* caused me to sink in my own Sea of Galilee.

What happened to my peace? I was feeling much better a moment ago. So I changed strategies. I counteracted prognosis with diplomas. In between paragraphs of bad news, I looked on the wall for reminders of good news.

That's what God wants us to do. His call to courage is not a call to naivete or ignorance. We aren't to be oblivious to the overwhelming challenges that life brings. We're to counterbalance them with long looks at God's accomplishments. "We must *pay much closer attention* to what we have heard, so that we do not drift away from it" (Heb. 2:1 NASB, emphasis mine). Do whatever it takes to keep your gaze on Jesus.

When a friend of mine spent several days in the hospital at the bedside of her husband, she relied on hymns to keep her spirits up. Every few minutes she stepped into the restroom and sang a few verses from "Great Is Thy Faithfulness." Do likewise! Memorize scripture. Read biographies of great lives. Ponder the testimonies of faithful Christians. Make the deliberate decision to set your hope on Jesus. Courage is always a possibility.

Feed your fears and your faith will starve.

Feed your faith and your fears will.

After a few moments of flailing in the water, Peter turned his focus back to Christ and cried, "'Lord, save me!' Immediately Jesus reached out his hand and caught him. 'You of little faith,' he said, 'why did you doubt?' And when they climbed into the boat, the wind died down" (Matt. 14:30–32).

Jesus could have stilled this storm hours earlier. But he didn't. He wanted to teach the followers a lesson. Jesus could have calmed your storm long ago too. But he hasn't. Does he also want to teach you a lesson? Could that lesson read something like this: "Storms are not optional, but fear is"?

God has hung his diplomas in the universe. Rainbows, sunsets, horizons, and star-sequined skies. He has recorded his accomplishments in Scripture. We're not talking six thousand hours of flight time. His résumé includes: Red Sea openings. Lions' mouths closings. Goliath topplings. Lazarus raisings. Storm stillings and strollings.

His lesson is clear. He's the commander of every storm. Are you scared in yours? Then stare at him.

Chapter 14

Your Faith Has
Made You Well

We don't know her name, but we know her situation. Her world was midnight black. Grope-in-the-dark-and-hope-for-help black. Read these three verses and see what I mean:

A large crowd followed Jesus and pushed very close around him. Among them was a woman who had been bleeding for twelve years. She had suffered very much from many doctors and had spent all the money she had, but instead of improving, she was getting worse. (Mark 5:24–26 NCV)

She was a bruised reed: "bleeding for twelve years," "suffered very much," "spent all the money she had," and "getting worse." She was physically exhausted and socially ostracized. She awoke daily in a body that no one wanted. She was down to her last prayer. And on the day we encounter her, she's about to pray it.

By the time she gets to Jesus, he is surrounded by people. He's on his way to help the daughter of Jairus, one of the most important men in the community. What are the odds that he will interrupt an urgent mission with a high official to help the likes of her? Still, she takes a chance.

"If I can just touch his clothes," she thinks, "I will be healed" (v. 28 NCV).

Risky decision. To touch him she will have to touch the people. If one of them recognizes her . . . hello rebuke, goodbye cure. But what choice does she have? She has no money, no clout, no friends, no solutions. All she has is a crazy hunch that Jesus can help and a high hope that he will.

Maybe that's all you have: a crazy hunch and a high hope. You have nothing to give. But you are hurting. And all you have to offer him is your hurt.

Maybe that has kept you from coming to God. Oh, you've taken a step or two in his direction. But then you saw the other people around him. They seemed so clean, so neat, so trim and fit in their faith. And when you saw them, they blocked your view of him. So you stepped back.

If that describes you, note carefully that only one person was commended that day for having faith. It wasn't a wealthy giver. It wasn't a loyal follower. It was a shame-struck, penniless outcast who clutched onto her hunch that he could help and her hope that he would.

Which, by the way, isn't a bad definition of faith: *a conviction that he can and a hope that he will*. Sounds similar to the definition of faith given in the Bible: "Without faith no one can please God. Anyone who comes to God must believe that he is real and that he rewards those who truly want to find him" (Heb. 11:6 NCV).

A healthy woman never would have appreciated the power of a touch of the hem of his robe. But this woman was sick, and when her dilemma met his dedication, a miracle occurred. Her part in the healing was very small. All she did was extend her arm through the crowd.

"If only I can touch him."

What's important is not the form of the effort but the fact of the effort. The fact is, she did something. She refused to settle for sickness another day and resolved to make a move.

Healing begins when we do something. Healing begins when we reach out. Healing starts when we take a step of faith.

God's help is near and always available, but it is given only to those who seek it. The great work in this story is the mighty healing that occurred. But the great truth is that the healing began with her touch. And with that small, courageous gesture, she experienced Jesus' tender power. "Jesus turned around, and when He saw her He said, 'Be of good cheer, daughter; your faith has made you well.' And the woman was made well from that hour" (Matt. 9:22 NKJV).

If you are low on faith but need the healing power of Christ, perhaps you could rely on the faith of a friend. This is the type of faith Jesus witnessed when he saw a man being lowered through a hole in the roof where Jesus was teaching one day (Mark 2:1–12).

Whether he was born paralyzed or became paralyzed, we don't know, but the end result was the same: total dependence on others. Someone had to wash his face and bathe his body. He couldn't blow his nose or go on a walk.

When people looked at him, they didn't see the man; they saw a body in need of a miracle. That's not what Jesus saw, but that's what the people saw. And that's certainly what his friends saw. So they did what any of us would do for a friend. They tried to get him some help.

Word was out that a carpenter-turned-teacher-turned-wonder-worker was in town. By the time his friends arrived at the place, the house was full. People jammed the doorways. Kids sat in the windows. Others peeked over shoulders. How would this small band of friends ever attract Jesus' attention? They had to make a choice: do we go in or give up?

What would have happened had the friends given up faith? What if they had shrugged their shoulders and mumbled something about the crowd being big and dinner getting cold and had turned and left? After all, they had done a good deed in coming this far. Who could fault them for turning back? You can do only so much for somebody. But these friends hadn't done enough.

One said he had an idea. The four huddled over the paralytic and discussed the plan to climb to the top of the house, cut through the roof, and lower their friend down with their sashes.

It was risky—they could fall. It was dangerous—he could fall. It was unorthodox—de-roofing is antisocial. It was intrusive—Jesus was busy. But it was their only chance to see Jesus. So they climbed to the roof.

Faith does those things. Faith does the unexpected. And faith gets God's attention. Look at what Mark says: "When Jesus saw the faith of these people, he said to the paralyzed man, 'Young man, your sins are forgiven'" (Mark 2:5 NCV).

Finally someone took Jesus at his word! Four men had enough hope in him and love for their friend that they took a chance. The stretcher above was a sign from above—somebody believes! Someone was willing to risk embarrassment and injury for just a few moments with the Galilean.

Jesus was moved by the scene of faith.

The request of the friends was valid—but timid. The expectations of the crowd were high—but not high enough. They expected Jesus to say, "I heal you." Instead he said, "I forgive you."

They expected him to treat the body, for that is what they saw.

He chose to treat not only the body but also the spirit, for that is what he saw.

They wanted Jesus to give the man a new body so he could walk. Jesus gave grace so the man could live. "And they were all amazed, and they glorified God" (Luke 5:26 NKJV).

Two pictures of miracle-prompting faith: A woman who reached out. Friends who drew near. Jesus responded both times. He did the impossible for them. He will do the same for you.

Chapter 15

The Wonder of Worship

*Jesus left there and went along the Sea of Galilee. Then
he went up on a mountainside and sat down. Great
crowds came to him, bringing the lame, the blind, the
crippled, the mute and many others, and laid them at
his feet; and he healed them. The people were amazed
when they saw the mute speaking, the crippled made
well, the lame walking and the blind seeing. And they
praised the God of Israel. (Matt. 15:29–31)*

Many times I've wished the New Testament writers had been
a bit more descriptive. This is one of those times. "And he
healed them" is too short a phrase to describe what must have been
an astonishing sight.

Let your imagination go. Can you see the scene?

Can you visualize the blind husband seeing his wife for the first time? His eyes gazing into her tear-filled ones as if she were the queen of the morning?

Envision the man who had never walked, now walking! Don't you know that he didn't want to sit down? Don't you know that he ran and jumped and did a dance with the kids?

For three days it went on. Person after person. Mat after mat. Crutch after crutch. Smile after smile. No record is given of Jesus preaching or teaching or instructing or challenging. He just healed.

Then Matthew, still the great economizer of words, gave us another phrase, on which I wish he would have elaborated: "They praised the God of Israel."

I wonder how they did that. I feel more certain of what they didn't do than of what they did do. I feel confident that they didn't form a praise committee. I feel confident that they didn't make any robes. I feel confident that they didn't sit in rows and stare at the back of each other's heads.

I doubt seriously that they wrote a creed on how they were to praise this Jesus they had never before worshiped. I can't picture them getting into an argument over technicalities. I doubt they felt their praise had to be done indoors.

And I know they didn't wait until the Sabbath to do it.

In all probability they just did it. Each one—in his or her own way, with his or her own heart—just praised Jesus. Perhaps some people came and fell at Jesus' feet. Perhaps some shouted his name. Maybe a few just went up on the hillside, looked into the sky, and smiled.

I can picture a mom and dad standing speechless before the Healer as they hold their newly healed baby.

I can envision a leper staring in awe at the One who took away his terror.

I can imagine throngs of people pushing and shoving, wanting to get close. Not to request anything or demand anything but just to say "thank you."

Perhaps some tried to pay Jesus, but what payment would have been sufficient?

Perhaps some tried to acknowledge his gift with their own gift, but what could a person give that would express the gratitude?

All that the people could do was exactly what Matthew said they did: "They praised the God of Israel."

However they did it, they did it. And Jesus was touched, so touched that he insisted they stay for a meal before they left.

Without using the word *worship*, this passage in Matthew 15 defines it.

Worship is when you're aware that what you've been given is far greater than what you can give. Worship is the awareness that were it not for his touch, you'd still be hobbling and hurting, bitter and broken. Worship is the half-glazed expression on the parched face of a desert pilgrim as he discovers that the oasis is not a mirage.

Worship is the "thank you" that refuses to be silenced.

We have tried to make a science out of worship. We can't do that. We can't do that any more than we can "sell love" or "negotiate peace."

Worship is a voluntary act of gratitude offered by the saved to the Savior—the kind of gratitude exhibited in the heart of the man born blind.

John introduces him to us with these words: "As [Jesus] passed by, He saw a man blind from birth" (John 9:1 NASB). This man has never seen a sunrise. Can't tell purple from pink. The disciples fault the family tree. "Rabbi, who sinned, this man or his parents, that he would be born blind?" (v. 2 NASB).

"Neither," the God-man replies. Trace this condition back to heaven. The reason the man was born sightless? So "the works of God might be displayed in him" (v. 3 NASB).

Talk about a thankless role. Selected to suffer. Some sing to God's glory. Others teach to God's glory. Who wants to be blind for God's glory? Which is tougher—having the condition or discovering it was God's idea?

The cure proves to be as surprising as the cause. "[Jesus] spat on the ground, and made clay of the spittle, and applied the clay to his eyes" (v. 6 NASB).

The world abounds with paintings of Jesus: in the arms of Mary, in the Garden of Gethsemane, in the Upper Room, in the darkened tomb. Jesus touching. Jesus weeping, laughing, teaching . . . But I've never seen a painting of Jesus spitting.

Christ smacking his lips a time or two, gathering a mouth of saliva, working up a blob of drool, and letting it go. Down in the dirt. (Kids, next time your mother tells you not to spit, show her this passage.) Then he squats, stirs up a puddle of . . . I don't know, what would you call it? Holy putty? Spit therapy? Saliva solution? Whatever the name, he places a fingerful in his palm, and then, as calmly as a painter spackles a hole in the wall, Jesus streaks mud-miracle on the blind man's eyes. "Go, wash in the pool of Siloam" (v. 7 NASB).

The beggar feels his way to the pool, splashes water on his mud-streaked face, and rubs away the clay. The result is the first chapter of Genesis just for him. Light where there was darkness. Virgin eyes focus, fuzzy figures become human beings, and John receives the Understatement of the Bible Award when he writes: "He . . . came back seeing" (v. 7 NASB).

Come on, John! Running short of verbs? How about "he *raced* back seeing"? "He *danced* back seeing"? "He *roared* back whooping and hollering and kissing everything he could—for the first time—see"? The guy had to be thrilled.

We would love to leave him that way, but if this man's life were a cafeteria line, he would have just stepped from the sirloin to the boiled brussels sprouts. Look at the reaction of the neighbors: "'Is not this the one who used to sit and beg?' Others were saying, 'This is he,' still others were saying, 'No, but he is like him.' He kept saying, 'I am the one'" (vv. 8–9 NASB).

These folks don't celebrate; they debate! They have watched this man grope and trip since he was a kid (v. 20). You'd think they would rejoice. But they don't. The Pharisees call him a heretic and cast him out of the synagogue.

"Jesus heard that they had thrown him out, and went and found him" (v. 35 THE MESSAGE). In case the stable birth wasn't enough, if three decades of earth walking and miracle working were insufficient, if there was any doubt regarding God's full-bore devotion, he does things like this. He tracks down a troubled pauper.

The beggar lifts his eyes to look into the face of the One who started all this. Jesus has one more question for him:

"Do you believe in the Son of God?"

He answered and said, "Who is He, Lord, that I may believe in Him?"

And Jesus said to him, "You have both seen Him and it is He who is talking with you."

Then he said, "Lord, I believe!" (vv. 35–38 NKJV)

John describes the final act of the once-blind man, and it is the only response you can have when you realize you are not looking into the face of a man but the face of God himself: "he worshiped Him" (v. 38 NASB).

Don't you know he knelt? Don't you think he wept? And how could he keep from wrapping his arms around the waist of the One who gave him sight? He worshiped him.

And one day when we are finally fully healed and standing in front of our Savior face-to-face, we will do the same. We will worship him.

PART 5

LAMB OF GOD

A person is not held accountable for operating-table thoughts. The same rule goes for dental chairs and delivery rooms. On any occasion when people stick needles in your arm, fingers in your mouth, or scalpels into your skin, the patient is not penalized for bizarre imaginings.

At least that is the justification I give to mine. As far as surgeries are concerned, this one was simple. As far as I'm concerned, however, no surgery that contains the word *cancer* is simple. Since my face has pockets of cancer, I have found myself spending horizontal time on the table of a doctor who specializes in extracting them.

He has a silky midnight-radio voice and likes to assure me that my cancer isn't serious. As he cuts on my temple, he says, "When it comes to cancer, you've got the best kind." Forgive me for not rejoicing. And forgive my tacky thinking. But during the second surgery, after the fourth or fifth reminder that I have a good cancer, here is what I thought—didn't say but thought: *Then why don't you take my cancer? Instead of cutting it out, take it in. Let's swap places. You take my cancer, and I'll take your knife.*

Of course I didn't say those words. Even in my drug-induced state, I knew better. Such transactions aren't allowed. You can't take my sickness. Nor can I take yours. You may give me your car or your cold, but your cancer? It's nontransferable.

If you have cancer in your body, you have to deal with it.

If you have cancer in your soul, however, Christ will take it for you. Not just take it from you. No, he'll take it for you.

Theologians call the act "substitutionary atonement." A simpler term might be "holy love."

To understand holy love, go to the Garden of Gethsemane. Surprised? You thought we'd go to the cross? We will. The cross is where we see the substitution, but the garden is where we feel it.

> Then Jesus went with them to the olive grove called Gethsemane, and he said, "Sit here while I go over there to pray." He took Peter and Zebedee's two sons, James and John, and he became anguished and distressed. He told them, "My soul is crushed with grief to the point of death. Stay here and keep watch with me."
>
> He went on a little farther and bowed with his face to the ground, praying, "My Father! If it is possible, let this cup of suffering be taken away from me. Yet I want your will to be done, not mine." (Matt. 26:36–39 NLT)

We've never seen Christ like this. Never heard such screams from his voice or seen such horror in his eyes. And never before has he told us: "My soul is crushed with grief to the point of death."

How is such emotion explained? What was Jesus fearing?

Christ feared a cup of suffering. *Cup*, in biblical terminology, is more than a utensil for drinking. *Cup* equals God's anger, judgment, and punishment. When God took pity on apostate Jerusalem, he said, "See, I have taken out of your hand the cup that made you stagger . . . the goblet of my wrath" (Isa. 51:22). According to John, those who dismiss God "must drink the wine of God's anger. It has been poured full strength into God's cup of wrath. And they will be tormented with fire and burning sulfur in the presence of the holy angels and the Lamb" (Rev. 14:10 NLT).

The *cup* equals God's wrath. Specifically, his anger toward our rebellion. We have ignored his Word, violated his standard. We have dismissed him. And he is angry.

Many have trouble with the idea of this anger. "Why the big fuss over a few mistakes?" some wonder. "Everyone messes up now and then." Everyone, that is, except God. He is holy. His holiness cannot turn a blind eye toward rebellion.

He feels the same way toward our sin that many of us felt toward the vandals who violated our church building. Some scoundrels broke into our sanctuary. They stole nothing. They took nothing. It was not their intent to rob; it was their intent to defame. Ascending the stairs to the baptistery, they wrote profanity on the wall and urinated on the towels.

My reaction to their actions was the same as yours: disgust, anger, disbelief. Do they know no reverence? The baptistery is a sacred place. The room is a blessed room. How dare anyone take the holy and use it for vulgarity?

How often has heaven asked the same question about us? Are not our bodies holy? Much more than a man-made baptistery, we are God-made temples. "Don't you know that your body is a temple of the Holy Spirit?" (1 Cor. 6:19 CEB). Our tongues, our hands, our brains are the dwelling place and tools of God. Yet when I use this tongue to hurt, these hands to injure, this brain for my glory and not God's, am I not vandalizing God's temple?

What you and I feel toward vandals is what God feels toward us. And, this is sobering, what those vandals deserve is what we deserve—punishment. My reaction was, "Put them in jail. Let them pay the price."

Never did I consider disguising myself as them and standing before the church and saying, "I'm the culprit. Punish me for my actions."

Those thoughts never entered my mind. But they entered the mind of God. For God is not only holy; he is also love. And holy love finds a way to punish the sin and love the scoundrel.

In the Garden of Gethsemane Jesus chose to do just that. Envision him on his knees amid the trees. Look long into the face of the One who looks long into heaven. Realize this: he is being handed a cup that bears your name. If he drinks it, God will do to him what God should do to you. If Christ drinks the cup, he will be your substitute.

And according to verse after verse in the Bible, Christ is willing to be just that:

For our sake he made him to be sin who knew no sin, so that in him we might become the righteousness of God. (2 Cor. 5:21 NRSV)

For Christ also died for sins once for all, the righteous for the unrighteous, that he might bring us to God. (1 Peter 3:18 RSV)

The Greek word *hyper* means "in place of" or "on behalf of." New Testament writers repeatedly turned to this preposition to describe the work of Christ:

Christ died for [hyper] our sins. (1 Cor. 15:3)

Christ redeemed us from the curse of the law by becoming a curse for [hyper] us. (Gal. 3:13)

Christ . . . gave himself for [hyper] our sins. (Gal. 1:3–4)

Jesus himself prophesied: "The good shepherd lays down his life for [hyper] the sheep." (John 10:11)

And "Greater love has no one than this, than to lay down one's life for his friends." (John 15:13 NKJV)

In the Upper Room Jesus took bread and explained, "This is my body given for [hyper] you" (Luke 22:19). And presenting the cup he explained, "This cup is the new covenant in my blood, which is poured out for [hyper] you" (Luke 22:20).

Forgive me for sounding hyper about *hyper*, but you need to see the point. The cross of Christ is more than a gift; it is a substitution. By taking the cup, Christ was taking our place. Though he did not vandalize, he was treated as a vandal. Though healthy, he was given our cancer. In the garden he agreed to take the full force of a sin-hating God.

Holy love does such things. If heaven were only holy and not love, we would be hopeless because of sin. If heaven were only love and not holy, the world would be chaos for lack of goodness. But since heaven is equally holy and loving, God himself saves us from himself. He punished the sin and saved the sinner by punishing the only sinless soul ever to live—Jesus Christ.

Let's thank him. Thank him with praise. Thank him with deeds. Thank him with worship and works of appreciation. He didn't have to take the cup. But he did. And since he did, you never will.

Chapter 16

God Saves

I have a sin nature.

So do you. Under the right circumstances you will do the wrong thing. You won't want to. You'll try not to, but you will. Why? You have a sin nature.

You were born with it. We all were. Our parents didn't teach us to throw temper tantrums; we were born with the skill. No one showed us how to steal a cookie from our sibling; we just knew. We never attended a class on pouting or passing the blame, but we could do both before we were out of our diapers.

Each one of us entered the world with a sin nature.

God entered the world to take it away. But it would come at great cost.

———

Look carefully at the words the angel spoke to Joseph.

Joseph son of David, do not be afraid to take Mary home as your wife, because what is conceived in her is from the Holy Spirit. She will give birth to a son, and you are to give him the name Jesus, because he will save his people from their sins. (Matt. 1:20–21)

We may not see the connection between the name *Jesus* and the phrase "save his people from their sins," but Joseph would have. He was familiar with the Hebrew language. The English name *Jesus* traces its origin to the Hebrew word *Yeshua*. *Yeshua* is a shortening of *Yehoshuah*, which means "Yahweh saves."

Who was Jesus? *God* saves.

What did Jesus come to do? God *saves*.

God saves, not God empathizes, cares, listens, helps, assists, or applauds. God saves. Specifically "he will save his people from their sins" (v. 21). Jesus came to save us, not just from politics, enemies, challenges, or difficulties. He came to save us from ourselves.

Here's why. God has high plans for you and me. He is recruiting for himself a people who will populate heaven. God will restore his planet and his children to their garden of Eden splendor. It will be perfect. Perfect in splendor. Perfect in righteousness. Perfect in harmony.

One word describes heaven: *perfect*.

One word describes us: *imperfect*.

God's kingdom is perfect, but his children are not, so what is he to do? Abandon us? Start over? He could. But he loves us too much to do that.

Will he tolerate us with our sin nature? Populate heaven with rebellious, self-centered citizens? If so, how would heaven be heaven?

It wouldn't. But God had a plan, a story he was writing from the beginning. The main character? Christ. The climax of the action? It began in the Upper Room.

> Jesus, knowing that the Father had given all things into His hands, and that He had come from God and was going to God, rose from supper and laid aside His garments, took a towel and girded Himself. After that, He poured water into a basin and began to wash the disciples' feet, and to wipe them with the towel with which He was girded. (John 13:3–5 NKJV)

This was the eve of the crucifixion and Jesus' final meal with his followers. John wanted us to know what Jesus knew. Jesus knew he had all authority. He knew he was sent from heaven. He knew he was destined for heaven. Jesus was certain about his identity and destiny. Because he knew who he was, he could do what he did.

He "rose from supper." When Jesus stood up, the disciples surely perked up. They may have thought Jesus was about to teach them something. He was, but not with words.

He then "laid aside His garments." Even the simple seamless garment of a rabbi was too ostentatious for the task at hand.

Jesus hung his cloak on a hook and girded the towel around his waist. He then took a pitcher of water and emptied it into a bowl. The only sound was the splash as Jesus filled the basin.

The next sound was the tap of the bowl as Jesus placed it on the floor. Then the shuffle of leather as he untied and removed the first of the two dozen sandals. There was more splashing as Jesus placed two feet, dirty as they were, into the water. He massaged the toes. He cupped crusty heels in his hands. He dried the feet with his towel. He then stood, emptied the basin of dirty water, filled it with fresh, and repeated the process on the next set of feet.

Splash. Wash. Massage. Dry.

How much time do you think this cleansing required? Supposing Jesus took two or three minutes per foot, this act would have taken the better part of an hour. Keep in mind, Jesus was down to his final minutes with his followers. If his three years with them were measured by sand in an hourglass, only a few grains had yet to fall. Jesus chose to use them in this silent sacrament of humility.

No one spoke. No one, that is, except Peter, who always had something to say. When he objected, Jesus insisted, going so far as to tell Peter, "If I do not wash you, you have no part with Me" (v. 8 NKJV).

Peter requested a bath.

Later that night the disciples realized the enormity of this gesture. They had pledged to stay with their Master, but those pledges melted like wax in the heat of the Roman torches. When the soldiers marched in, the disciples ran out.

I envision them sprinting until, depleted of strength, they plopped to the ground and let their heads fall forward as they looked wearily at the dirt. That's when they saw the feet Jesus had just washed. That's when they realized he had given them grace before they even knew they needed it.

Jesus forgave his betrayers before they betrayed him.

He didn't exclude a single follower, though we wouldn't have faulted him had he bypassed Philip. When Jesus told the disciples to feed the throng of five thousand hungry people, Philip retorted, "It's impossible!" (John 6:7, paraphrased). So what does Jesus do with someone who questions his commands? Apparently he washes the doubter's feet.

James and John lobbied for cabinet-level positions in Christ's kingdom. So what does Jesus do when people use his kingdom for personal advancement? He slides a basin in their direction.

Peter quit trusting Christ in the storm. He tried to talk Christ out of going to the cross. Within hours Peter would curse the very name of Jesus and hightail his way into hiding. In fact, all twenty-four of Jesus' followers' feet would soon scoot, leaving Jesus to face his accusers alone. Do you ever wonder what God does with promise breakers? He washes their feet.

And Judas. The lying, conniving, greedy rat who sold Jesus down the river for a pocket of cash. Jesus wouldn't wash his feet, would he? Sure hope not. If he washed the feet of his Judas, you will have to wash the feet of yours. Your betrayer. Your turkey-throwing misfit and miscreant. That ne'er-do-well, that good-for-nothing villain. Jesus' Judas walked away with thirty pieces of silver. Your Judas walked away with your security, spouse, job, childhood, retirement, investments.

You expect me to wash his feet and let him go?

Most people don't want to. They use the villain's photo as a dartboard. Their Vesuvius erupts every now and again, sending hate airborne, polluting and stinking the world. Most people keep a pot of anger on low boil.

But you aren't "most people." Grace has happened to you. Look at your feet. They are wet, grace soaked. Your toes and arches and heels have felt the cool basin of God's grace. Jesus has washed the grimiest parts of your life. He didn't bypass you and carry the basin toward someone else. If grace were a wheat field, he's bequeathed you the state of Kansas. Can't you share your grace with others?

"Since I, your Lord and Teacher, have washed your feet, you ought to wash each other's feet. I have given you an example to follow. Do as I have done to you" (John 13:14–15 NLT).

If you think washing the disciples' feet was the ultimate act of servitude, just wait. It was only the beginning. The hours that followed hold the most remarkable example of service, humility, and sacrifice that Jesus' followers, and anyone since, have ever seen.

It was nearly midnight when they left the Upper Room and descended through the streets of the city. They passed the Lower Pool and exited the Fountain Gate and walked out of Jerusalem. The roads were lined with the fires and tents of Passover pilgrims. Most were asleep, heavied with the evening meal. Those still awake thought little of the band of men walking the chalky road.

They passed through the valley and ascended the path that would take them to Gethsemane. The road was steep, so they stopped to rest. Somewhere within the city walls the twelfth apostle darted down a street. His feet had been washed by the man he would betray. His heart had been claimed by the evil one he had heard. He ran to find Caiaphas.

The final encounter of the battle had begun.

As Jesus looked at the city of Jerusalem, he saw what the disciples couldn't. It is here, on the outskirts of Jerusalem, that the battle would end. He saw the staging of Satan. He saw the dashing of the demons. He saw the evil one preparing for the final encounter. The Enemy lurked as a specter over the hour. Satan, the host of hatred, had seized the heart of Judas and whispered in the ear of Caiaphas. Satan, the master of death, had opened the caverns and prepared to receive the source of light.

Hell was breaking loose.

History records it as a battle of the Jews against Jesus. It wasn't. It was a battle of God against Satan.

And Jesus knew it. He knew that before the war was over, he would be taken captive. He knew that before victory would come defeat. He knew that before he sat on the throne again, he would have to drink the cup. He knew that before the light of Sunday would come the blackness of Friday.

And he was afraid . . .

Never had he felt so alone. What must be done, only he could do. An angel couldn't do it. No angel has the power to break open hell's gates. A human couldn't do it. No human has the purity to destroy sin's claim. No force on earth can face the force of evil and win—except God.

"The spirit is willing, but the flesh is weak," Jesus confessed (Mark 14:38). His humanity begged to be delivered from what his divinity could see. Jesus, the carpenter, implored. Jesus, the man, peered into the dark pit and begged, "Can't there be another way?"

Did he know the answer before he asked the question? Did his human heart hope his heavenly Father had found another way? We don't know. But we do know he asked to get out. We do know he begged for an exit. We do know there was a time when he could have turned his back on the whole mess and gone away.

But he didn't.

He didn't because he saw you right there in the middle of a world that isn't fair. He saw you cast into a river of life you didn't request. He saw you betrayed by those you love. He saw you with a body that gets sick and a heart that grows weak.

He saw you in your own garden of gnarled trees and sleeping friends. He saw you staring into the pit of your own failures and the mouth of your own grave.

He saw you in your Garden of Gethsemane—and he didn't want you to be alone.

He wanted you to know that he has been there too. He knows what it's like to be plotted against. He knows what it's like to be conflicted. He knows what it's like to be torn between two desires. He knows what it's like to smell the stench of Satan. And, perhaps most of all, he knows what it's like to beg God to change his mind and to hear God say so gently, but firmly, "No."

For that is what God said to Jesus. And Jesus accepted the answer. At some moment during that midnight hour, an angel of mercy came over the weary body of the man in the garden. As he stood, the anguish was gone from his eyes. His fist would clench no more. His heart would fight no more.

The battle was won. You may have thought it was won on Golgotha. It wasn't. You may have thought the sign of victory was the empty tomb. It wasn't. The final battle was won in Gethsemane. And the sign of conquest was Jesus at peace in the olive trees.

For it was in the garden that he made his decision. He would rather go to hell for you than go to heaven without you.

Around nine o'clock the next morning, Jesus stumbled to the

cleft of Skull Hill. A soldier pressed a knee on his forearm and drove a spike through one hand, then the other, then both feet. As the Romans lifted the cross, they unwittingly placed Christ in the very position in which he came to die—between humanity and God.

A priest on his own altar.

Noises intermingled on the hill: Pharisees mocking, swords clanging, and dying men groaning. Jesus scarcely spoke. When he did, diamonds sparkled against velvet. He gave his killers grace and his mother a son. He answered the prayer of a thief and asked for a drink from a soldier.

Then, at midday, darkness fell like a curtain. "At noon the whole country was covered with darkness, which lasted for three hours" (Matt. 27:45 GNT).

This was a supernatural darkness, not a casual gathering of clouds or a brief eclipse of the sun. This was a three-hour blanket of blackness. Merchants in Jerusalem lit candles. Soldiers ignited torches. Parents worried. People everywhere asked, "From whence comes this noonday night?" As far away as Egypt, the historian Dionysius took notice of the black sky and wrote, "Either the God of nature is suffering, or the machine of the world is tumbling into ruin."[1]

Of course the sky was dark; people were killing the Light of the World.

The universe grieved as God said it would. "On that day . . . I will make the sun go down at noon, and darken the earth in broad daylight. . . . I will make it like the mourning for an only son, and the end of it like a bitter day" (Amos 8:9–10 RSV).

The sky wept. And a lamb bleated. Remember the time of the

scream? "At about three o'clock, Jesus called out" (Matt. 27:46 NLT). Three o'clock in the afternoon, the hour of the temple sacrifice. Less than a mile to the east a finely clothed priest led a lamb to the slaughter, unaware that his work was futile. Heaven was not looking at the lamb of man but at "the Lamb of God, who takes away the sin of the world" (John 1:29 RSV).

Chapter 17

"It Is Finished"

*A*bandon. Such a haunting word.

Abandoned by family.

Abandoned by a spouse.

Abandoned by big business.

But nothing compares to being abandoned by God.

"Jesus cried out with a loud voice" (Matt. 27:46 NASB). Note the sturdy words here. Other writers employed the Greek word for "loud voice" to describe a "roar."[1] Soldiers aren't cupping an ear, asking him to speak up. The Lamb roars. "The sun and the moon shall be darkened. . . . The LORD also shall roar out of Zion, and utter his voice from Jerusalem" (Joel 3:15–16 KJV).

Christ lifts his heavy head and eyelids toward the heavens and spends his final energy crying out toward the ducking stars. "'*Eli, Eli, lema sabachthani?*' which means, 'My God, my God, why did you abandon me?'" (Matt. 27:46 GNT).

We would ask the same. Why him? Why forsake your Son? Forsake the murderers. Desert the evildoers. Turn your back on perverts and peddlers of pain. Abandon them, not him. Why would you abandon earth's only sinless soul?

Ah, there is the hardest word. *Abandon.* The house no one wants. The child no one claims. The parent no one remembers. The Savior no one understands. He pierces the darkness with heaven's loneliest question: "My God, my God, why did you abandon me?"

Wait a second. Didn't David tell us, "I have never seen the righteous forsaken" (Ps. 37:25)? Did David misspeak? Did Jesus misstep? Neither. In this hour Jesus is anything but righteous. But his mistakes aren't his own. "Christ carried our sins in his body on the cross so we would stop living for sin and start living for what is right" (1 Peter 2:24 NCV).

Christ carried all our sins in his body . . .

Suppose your past sins were made public? Suppose you were to stand on a stage while a film of every secret and selfish second was projected on the screen behind you?

Would you not crawl beneath the rug? Would you not scream for the heavens to have mercy? And would you not feel just a fraction . . . just a fraction of what Christ felt on the cross? The icy displeasure of a sin-hating God?

Christ carried all our sins in his body.

See Christ on the cross? That's a gossiper hanging there. See Jesus? Embezzler. Liar. Bigot. See the crucified carpenter? He's a wife beater.

Porn addict and murderer. See Bethlehem's boy? Call him by his other names—Adolf Hitler, Osama bin Laden, and Jeffrey Dahmer.

Hold it, Max. Don't lump Christ with those evildoers. Don't place his name in the same sentence with theirs!

I didn't. *He* did. Indeed he did more. More than place his name in the same sentence, he placed himself in their place. And yours. With hands nailed open he invited God, "Treat me as you would treat them!" And God did. In an act that broke the heart of the Father, yet honored the holiness of heaven, sin-purging judgment flowed over the sinless Son of the ages. Everything the story had been building to landed at this moment with one final phrase.

Stop and listen. Can you imagine the final cry from the cross? The sky is dark. The other two victims are moaning. The jeering mouths are silent. Perhaps there is thunder. Perhaps there is weeping. Perhaps there is silence. Then Jesus draws a deep breath, pushes his feet down on that Roman nail, and cries, "It is finished!" (John 19:30 NKJV).

What was finished?

Our inability to finish what we start is seen in the smallest of things:

A partly mowed lawn
A half-read book
Letters begun but never completed
An abandoned diet
A car up on blocks

And it shows up in life's most painful areas:

An abandoned child
A cold faith
A job hopper
A wrecked marriage
An unevangelized world

Am I touching some painful sores? Any chance I'm addressing someone who is considering giving up? If I am, I want to encourage you to remain. I want to encourage you to remember Jesus' determination on the cross.

Jesus didn't quit. But don't think for one minute that he wasn't tempted to. Watch him wince as he hears his apostles backbite and quarrel. Look at him weep as he sits at Lazarus's tomb, or hear him wail as he claws the ground of Gethsemane.

Did he ever want to quit? You bet.

That's why his words are so splendid.

"It is finished."

The history-long plan of redeeming humanity was finished. The message of God to humans was finished. The works done by Jesus as a man on earth were finished. The task of selecting and training ambassadors was finished. The job was finished. The song had been sung. The blood had been poured. The sacrifice had been made. The sting of death had been removed. It was over. A cry of defeat? Hardly. Had his hands not been fastened down, I dare say that a triumphant fist would have punched the dark sky. No, this was not a cry of despair. It was a cry of completion. A cry of victory. A cry of fulfillment. Yes, even a cry of relief.

The fighter remained. And thank God that he did. Thank God

that he endured, because you cannot deal with your own sins. "Only God can forgive sins" (Mark 2:7 NCV). Jesus is "the Lamb of God, who takes away the sin of the world!" (John 1:29 NCV).

How did God deal with your debt?

Did he overlook it? He could have. He could have burned the statement. He could have ignored your bounced checks. But would a holy God do that? *Could* a holy God do that? No. He wouldn't be holy. Besides, is that how we want God to run his world—ignoring our sin and thereby endorsing our rebellion?

Did he punish you for your sins? Again, he could have. He could have crossed out your name in the book and wiped you off the face of the earth. But would a loving God do that? Could a loving God do that? He loves you with an everlasting love. Nothing can separate you from his love.

So what did he do? "God put the world square with himself through the Messiah, giving the world a fresh start by offering forgiveness of sins. . . . How? you ask. In Christ. God put the wrong on him who never did anything wrong, so we could be put right with God" (2 Cor. 5:19–21 THE MESSAGE).

The cross included a "putting on." God put our wrong on Christ so he could put Christ's righteousness on us.

Something remotely similar happened to me at a restaurant. The maître d' tried to turn me away. He didn't care that Denalyn and I were on our honeymoon. It didn't matter that the evening at the classy country club restaurant was a wedding gift. He couldn't have cared less that Denalyn and I had gone without lunch to save room for dinner. All of this was immaterial in comparison to the looming problem.

I wasn't wearing a jacket.

I didn't know I needed one. I thought a sport shirt was sufficient. It was clean and tucked in. But Mr. Black-Tie with the French accent was unimpressed. He seated everyone else. Mr. and Mrs. Debonair were given a table. Mr. and Mrs. Classier-Than-You were seated. But Mr. and Mrs. Didn't-Wear-a-Jacket?

If I'd had another option, I wouldn't have begged. But I didn't. The hour was late. Other restaurants were closed or booked, and we were hungry. "There's got to be something you can do," I pleaded. He looked at me, then at Denalyn, and let out a long sigh that puffed his cheeks.

"All right, let me see."

He disappeared into the cloakroom and emerged with a jacket. "Put this on." I did. The sleeves were too short. The shoulders were too tight. And the color was lime green. But I didn't complain. I had a jacket, and we were taken to a table. (Don't tell anyone, but I took it off when the food came.)

For all the inconvenience of the evening, we ended up with a great dinner and an even greater parable.

I needed a jacket, but all I had was a prayer. The fellow was too kind to turn me away but too loyal to lower the standard. So the very one who required a jacket gave me a jacket, and we were given a table.

Isn't this what happened at the cross? Seats at God's table are not available to the sloppy. But who among us is anything but? Unkempt morality. Untidy with truth. Careless with people. Our moral clothing is in disarray. Yes, the standard for sitting at God's table is high, but the love of God for his children is higher.

So he offers a gift. Not a lime-colored jacket but a robe. A seamless robe. Not a garment pulled out of a cloakroom but a robe worn by his Son, Jesus.

The character of Jesus was a seamless fabric woven from heaven to earth . . . from God's thoughts to Jesus' actions. From God's tears to Jesus' compassion. From God's word to Jesus' response. All one piece. All a picture of the character of Jesus. But when Christ was nailed to the cross, he took off his robe of seamless perfection and assumed a different wardrobe, the wardrobe of indignity.

The indignity of nakedness. Stripped before his own mother and loved ones. Shamed before his family.

The indignity of failure. For a few pain-filled hours, the religious leaders were the victors, and Christ appeared the loser. Shamed before his accusers.

Worst of all, he wore *the indignity of sin.* "'He himself bore our sins' in his body on the cross, so that we might die to sins and live for righteousness" (1 Peter 2:24).

The clothing of Christ on the cross? Sin—yours and mine. The sins of all humanity.

I can remember my father explaining to me the reason a group of men on the side of the road wore striped clothing. "They're prisoners," he said. "They have broken the law and are serving time."

You want to know what stuck with me about these men? They never looked up. They never made eye contact. Were they ashamed? Probably so.

What they felt on the side of the road was what our Savior felt on the cross—disgrace. Every aspect of the crucifixion was intended not only to hurt the victim but to shame him. Death on a cross was usually reserved for the most vile offenders: murderers, assassins, and the like. The condemned person was marched through the city streets, shouldering his crossbar and wearing a placard about his neck that named his crime. At the execution site he was stripped and mocked.

Crucifixion was so abhorrent that Cicero wrote, "Let the very name of the cross be far away, not only from the body of a Roman citizen, but even from his thoughts, his eyes, his ears."[2] Jesus was not only shamed before people, he was shamed before heaven.

Since he bore the sin of the murderer and adulterer, he felt the shame of the murderer and adulterer. Though he never lied, he bore the disgrace of a liar. Though he never cheated, he felt the embarrassment of a cheater. Since he bore the sin of the world, he felt the collective shame of the world.

It's no wonder that the writer of Hebrews spoke of the "disgrace he bore" (Heb. 13:13 NLT).

While on the cross, Jesus felt the indignity and disgrace of a criminal. No, he was not guilty. No, he had not committed a sin. And no, he did not deserve to be sentenced. But you and I were, we had, and we did. We were left in the same position I was with the maître d´—having nothing to offer but a prayer. Jesus, however, goes further than the maître d´. Can you imagine the restaurant host removing his tuxedo coat and offering it to me?

Jesus does. We're not talking about an ill-fitting, leftover jacket. He offers a robe of seamless purity and dons my patchwork coat of pride, greed, and selfishness. "He changed places with us" (Gal. 3:13 NCV). He wore our sin so we could wear his righteousness.

Though we come to the cross dressed in sin, we leave the cross dressed in the "coat of his strong love" (Isa. 59:17 NCV) and girded with a belt of "goodness and fairness" (Isa. 11:5 NCV) and clothed in "garments of salvation" (Isa. 61:10).

Indeed, we leave dressed in Christ himself. "You have all put on Christ as a garment" (Gal. 3:27 NEB).

It wasn't enough for him to prepare you a feast.

It wasn't enough for him to reserve you a seat.

It wasn't enough for him to cover the cost and provide the transportation to the banquet.

He did something more. He let you wear his own clothes so you would be properly dressed.

"With one sacrifice [Jesus] made perfect forever those who are being made holy" (Heb. 10:14 NCV). No more sacrifice needs to be made. No more deposits are necessary. So complete was the payment that Jesus used a banking term to proclaim your salvation. "It is finished!" (John 19:30 NKJV). *Tetelestai* (It is finished) was a financial term used to announce the final installment, the ultimate payment.

Now, if the task is finished, is anything else required of you? Of course not. If the account is full, what more could you add?

PART 6

RETURNING KING

The most luxurious flight in the world is offered by Etihad Airways, the United Arab Emirates national carrier. They will fly you from New York City to Mumbai in your own "penthouse in the sky." It comes with a chef, a butler, and turndown service for the double bed that is outfitted with Italian linens. You will enjoy your private living room and relax on a leather couch as you binge-watch movies on your thirty-two-inch flat-screen television. Meals are cooked to order and served in abundance. Before landing, if you choose, you can take a shower in your private bathroom and make dinner arrangements through your personal concierge.[1]

I would like to experience the flight. I don't want to pay the $38,000 one-way ticket, but if given the opportunity free of charge, I'd take it. And I would have only one stipulation. The flight needs to end. I don't care how wonderful, opulent, luxurious, and magnificent the flight is; I really want it to end.

I enjoy the journey as much as the next person. I just don't want the journey to last forever. You don't either. We were wired to seek a destination. We are human homing pigeons. Something inside us longs to land at our intended destination.

Perhaps that is why we cherish thinking of Jesus as our Returning King. He gives us this encouragement:

Hold on to your faith in God and to your faith in me. There are many rooms in my Father's House. If there were not, should I have told you that I am going to prepare a place for you? It is true that I am going away to prepare a place for you, but it is just as true that I am coming again to welcome you into my own home, so that you may be where I am. (John 14:1–3 PHILLIPS)

Underline that promise and highlight it in yellow: "I am coming again." Christ guarantees his second coming. This return visit will be for good. For our good. He urges us to prepare for and ponder often the world that awaits us.

"Set your mind on things above" (Col. 3:2 NKJV). This verb emerges from the verb *phroneo*, which means "to savor or think about," causing one translation to read "Set your affection on things above" (KJV).

I obeyed this passage in an earthly fashion. Months before we moved to San Antonio in 1988, I knew what our house looked like. It was a brick house with a dark brown door on a quiet cul-de-sac. Before we moved to the United States from Rio, some friends sent us a picture of the house. It was for sale. And with one look I was sold. I posted the photo in our Brazilian kitchen and gave it multiple gazes a day. I studied its exterior and pondered its interior. I showed the photo to the girls and examined it with my wife. By the time we moved to San Antonio, I could have picked out the house from a dozen others. I was acquainted with my home before I reached it.

Christ wants us to do the same. He has changed our permanent residence. "Think only about" it (NCV). "Keep your mind" on it (GW). "Think about the things of heaven" (NLT). "Pursue the things over which Christ presides" (THE MESSAGE). These translations combine to declare in one verse: obsess yourself with the life to come!

Heaven is the green vegetable on the spiritual diet. The soul needs hourly gazes into our forever home. You need to know that Christ is coming for you. You need to know what your eternal body will be like. You need to imagine the New Jerusalem and the face of God. You need to be consumed with things above.

Not easy to do. Heaven-focus demands diligence. This life is full of distractions and detours. But don't heed them. Listen to your heart.

In C. S. Lewis's *The Voyage of the Dawn Treader*, Reepicheep, the valiant mouse, resolves to discover Aslan's country. "While I can," he declares, "I sail east in the *Dawn Treader*. When she fails me, I paddle east in my coracle. When she sinks, I shall swim east with my four paws. And when I can swim no longer, if I have not reached Aslan's country, or shot over the edge of the world in some vast cataract, I shall sink with my nose to the sunrise."[2]

May God stir identical hunger in us. May we seek those things that are above, set our minds on things above. May we sail, paddle, swim, and, if need be, die with our noses to the sunrise, savoring the day we will finally be home.

—————

Chapter 18

The Resurrection and the Life

You are leaving the church building. The funeral is over. The burial is next. Ahead of you walk six men who carry the coffin that carries the body of your son. Your only son.

You're numb from the sorrow. Stunned. You lost your husband, and now you've lost your son. Now you have no family. If you had any more tears, you'd weep. If you had any more faith, you'd pray. But both are in short supply, so you do neither. You just stare at the back of the wooden box.

Suddenly it stops. The pallbearers have stopped. You stop.

A man has stepped in front of the casket. You don't know him.

You've never seen him. He wasn't at the funeral. He's dressed in a corduroy coat and jeans. You have no idea what he is doing. But before you can object, he steps up to you and says, "Don't cry."

Don't cry? Don't cry! This is a funeral. My son is dead. Don't cry? Who are you to tell me not to cry? Those are your thoughts, but they never become your words. Because before you can speak, he acts.

He turns back to the coffin, places his hand on it, and says in a loud voice, "Young man, I tell you, get up!"

"Now just a minute," one of the pallbearers objects. But the sentence is interrupted by a sudden movement in the casket. The men look at one another and lower it quickly to the ground. It's a good thing they do, because as soon as it touches the sidewalk, the lid slowly opens.

Sound like something out of a science fiction novel? It's not. It's right out of the gospel of Luke. "He went up and touched the coffin, and the people who were carrying it stopped. Jesus said, 'Young man, I tell you, get up!' And the son sat up and began to talk" (Luke 7:14–15 NCV).

Be careful now. Don't read that last line too fast. Try it again. Slowly.

"The son sat up and began to talk."

Incredible sentence, don't you think? At the risk of overdoing it, let's read it one more time. This time say each word aloud. "The son sat up and began to talk."

Good job. (Did everyone around you look up?) Can we do it again? This time read it aloud again, but very s-l-o-w-l-y. Pause after each word.

"The . . . son . . . sat . . . up . . . and . . . began . . . to . . . talk."

Now the question. What's odd about that verse?

You got it. Dead people don't sit up! Dead people don't talk! Dead people don't leave their coffins!

Unless Jesus shows up. Because when Jesus shows up, you never know what might happen.

Jairus can tell you. His daughter was already dead. The mourners were already in the house. The funeral had begun. The people thought the best Jesus could do was offer some kind words about Jairus's girl. Jesus had some words all right. Not about the girl, but for the girl. "My child, stand up!" (Luke 8:54 NCV).

The next thing the father knew, she was eating, Jesus was laughing, and the hired mourners were sent home early.

Martha experienced a similar miracle. She'd hoped Jesus would show up to heal Lazarus. He didn't. Then she'd hoped he'd show up to bury Lazarus. He didn't. By the time he made it to Bethany, Lazarus was four-days buried, and Martha was wondering what kind of friend Jesus was. She hears he's at the edge of town, so she storms out to meet him. "Lord, if you had been here," she confronts, "my brother would not have died" (John 11:21 NCV).

There is hurt in those words. Hurt and disappointment. The one man who could have made a difference didn't, and Martha wants to know why.

Maybe you do too. Maybe you've done what Martha did. Someone you love ventures near the edge of life, and you turn to Jesus for help. You, like Martha, turn to the only one who can pull a person from the ledge of death. You ask Jesus to give a hand.

Martha must have thought, *Surely he will come. Didn't he aid the paralytic? Didn't he help the leper? Didn't he give sight to the blind? And they hardly knew Jesus. Lazarus is his friend. We're like family. Doesn't Jesus come for the weekend? Doesn't he eat at our table? When he hears that Lazarus is sick, he'll be here in a heartbeat.*

But he didn't come. Lazarus got worse. She watched out the window. Jesus didn't show. Her brother drifted in and out of consciousness. "He'll be here soon, Lazarus," she promised. "Hang on."

But the knock at the door never came. Jesus never appeared. Not to help. Not to heal. Not to bury. And now, four days later, he finally shows up. The funeral is over. The body is buried, and the grave is sealed. "If only you had been here," she told Jesus, "my brother would not have died" (v. 21 NLT).

Something about death makes us accuse God of betrayal. "If God were here, there would be no death!" we claim.

If God is God anywhere, he has to be God in the face of death. Pop psychology can deal with depression. Pep talks can deal with pessimism. Prosperity can handle hunger. But only God can deal with our ultimate dilemma—death. And only the God of the Bible has dared to stand on the canyon's edge and offer an answer. He has to be God in the face of death. If not, he is not God anywhere.

Jesus wasn't angry at Martha. Perhaps it was his patience that caused her to change her tone from frustration to earnestness. "Even now God will give you whatever you ask" (v. 22).

Jesus then made one of those claims that place him either on the throne or in the asylum: "Your brother will rise again" (v. 23).

Martha misunderstood. (Who wouldn't have?) "I know he will rise again in the resurrection at the last day" (v. 24).

That wasn't what Jesus meant. Don't miss the context of the next words. Imagine the setting: Jesus has intruded on the Enemy's turf; he's standing in Satan's territory, Death Canyon. His stomach turns as he smells the sulfuric stench of the ex-angel, and he winces as he hears the oppressed wails of those trapped in the prison. Satan has been here. He has violated one of God's creations.

With his foot planted on the Serpent's head, Jesus speaks loudly enough that his words echo off the canyon walls. "I am the resurrection and the life. The one who believes in me will live, even though they die; and whoever lives by believing in me will never die" (vv. 25–26).

It is a hinge point in history. A chink has been found in death's armor. The keys to the halls of hell have been claimed. The buzzards scatter and the scorpions scurry as Life confronts death—and wins! The wind stops. A cloud blocks the sun, and a bird chirps in the distance while a humiliated snake slithers between the rocks and disappears into the ground.

"Lazarus, come out!" (v. 43).

Martha is silent. The mourners are quiet. No one stirs as Jesus stands face-to-face with the rock-hewn tomb and demands that it release his friend.

No one stirs, that is, except Lazarus. Deep within the tomb he moves. His stilled heart begins to beat again. Wrapped eyes pop open. Wooden fingers lift. And a mummied man in a tomb sits up. Want to know what happened next?

Let John tell you. "The dead man came out, his hands and feet wrapped with strips of linen, and a cloth around his face" (v. 44).

Question: What's wrong with this picture?

Answer: Dead people don't walk out of tombs.

Question: What kind of God is this?

Answer: The God who holds the keys to life and death.

Can Jesus actually replace death with life? He did a convincing job with his own.

Fast-forward to the Sunday morning after the Friday crucifixion of Jesus. Joy is the last thing Mary Magdalene expects as she approaches the tomb. The last few days had brought nothing to celebrate. The Jews could celebrate—Jesus was out of the way. The soldiers could celebrate—their work was done. But Mary couldn't celebrate. To her the last few days had brought nothing but tragedy.

Mary had been there. She had heard the leaders clamor for Jesus' blood. She had witnessed the Roman whip rip the skin off his back. She had winced as the thorns sliced his brow and had wept at the weight of the cross.

She was there. She was there to place her arm around the shoulders of Mary the mother of Jesus. She was there to close his eyes. She was there.

So it's not surprising that she wants to be there again.

In the early morning mist she arises from her mat, takes her spices and aloes, leaves her house, and walks past the Gate of Gennath and up to the hillside. She anticipates a somber task. By now the body will be swollen. His face will be white. Death's odor will be pungent.

A gray sky gives way to gold as she walks up the narrow trail. As she rounds the final bend, she gasps. The rock in front of the grave is pushed back.

Someone took the body. She runs to awaken Peter and John.

They rush to see for themselves. She tries to keep up with them but can't.

Peter comes out of the tomb bewildered, and John comes out believing, but Mary just sits in front of it weeping. The two men go home and leave her alone with her grief.

But something tells her she is not alone. Maybe she hears a noise. Maybe she hears a whisper. Or maybe she just hears her own heart telling her to look for herself.

Whatever the reason, she does. She stoops down, sticks her head into the hewn entrance, and waits for her eyes to adjust to the dark.

She hears, "Why are you crying?" (John 20:13), and she sees what look to be two angels, because they're white—radiantly white. They are two lights on either end of the vacant slab. Two candles blazing on an altar.

"Why are you crying?" An uncommon question to be asked in a cemetery. In fact, the question is rude. That is, unless the questioner knows something the questionee doesn't.

"They have taken my Lord away, and I don't know where they have put him" (v. 13).

She still calls him "my Lord." As far as she knows, his lips are silent. As far as she knows, his corpse has been carted off by grave robbers. But in spite of it all, he is still her Lord. Such devotion moves Jesus. It moves him closer to her. So close she hears him breathing. She turns and there he stands. She thinks he is the gardener.

"Why are you crying?" he asks. "Who is it you are looking for?" (v. 15).

Thinking the gardener knows the location of the body, she asks him to tell her. She will fetch the corpse. But then Jesus speaks.

"Mary" (v. 16).

Mary was shocked. It's not often you hear your name spoken by an eternal tongue. But when she did, she recognized it. And when she did, she responded correctly. She worshiped him. In a moment she realized the truth of the gospel that had yet to spread: the resurrection, not of Lazarus, but of Christ himself.

Friday's tragedy emerged as Sunday's Savior, and even Satan knew he'd been had. He'd been a tool in the hand of the Gardener. All the time he thought he was defeating heaven, he was helping heaven. God wanted to prove his power over sin and death, and that's exactly what he did. And guess who helped him do it? Once again Satan's layup became a foul-up. Only this time he didn't give heaven some points; he gave heaven the championship game.

"Death has been swallowed up in victory" (1 Cor. 15:54).

Chapter 19

The Great Day

With hopes of earning extra cash, my dad once took a three-month job assignment in New England. I was ten years old, midway between training wheels and girlfriends. I thought much about baseball and bubble gum. Can't say I ever thought once about Bangor, Maine. Until Dad went there.

When he did, I found the town on the map. I calculated the distance between the Texas plains and the lobster coast. My teacher let me write a report on Henry Wadsworth Longfellow, and Dad sent us a jug of maple syrup. Our family lived in two worlds, ours and his.

We talked much about my father's pending return. "When Dad comes back, we will fix the basketball net . . . take a trip to

Grandma's . . . stay up later." Mom used his coming to comfort and caution. She could do both with the same phrase. With soft assurance: "Your dad will be home soon." Or clenched teeth: "Your dad will be home soon." She circled his arrival date on the calendar and crossed out each day as it passed. She made it clear: Dad's coming would be a big deal.

It was. Four decades have weathered the memories, but these remain: the sudden smell of Old Spice in the house; his deep, bellowing voice; gifts all around; and a happy sense of settledness. Dad's return changed everything.

The return of Christ will do likewise.

Jude has a name for this event: "the great day" (Jude v. 6 NKJV). The phrase fits. Everything about the day will be unprecedented. His shout will get our attention. "For the Lord Himself will descend from heaven with a shout" (1 Thess. 4:16 NKJV). Before we see angels, hear trumpets, or embrace our grandparents, we will be engulfed by Jesus' voice. John heard the voice of God and compared it to "the sound of many waters" (Rev. 1:15 NKJV). Perhaps you've stood at the base of a cataract so loud and full of fury that you had to shout to be heard. Or maybe you've heard the roar of a lion. When the king of beasts opens his mouth, every head in the jungle lifts. The King of kings will prompt the same response: "The LORD will roar from on high" (Jer. 25:30 NKJV).

Lazarus heard such a roar. His body was entombed and his soul in paradise when Jesus shouted into both places. "[Jesus] cried with a loud voice, 'Lazarus, come forth!' And he who had died came out" (John 11:43–44 NKJV). Expect the same shout and shaking of the corpses on the Great Day. "The dead will hear the voice of the

Son of God. . . . All who are . . . in their graves will hear his voice. Then they will come out" (John 5:25, 28–29 NCV).

The shout of God will trigger the "voice of an archangel . . . with the trumpet of God" (1 Thess. 4:16 NKJV). The archangel is the commanding officer. He will dispatch armies of angels to their greatest mission: to gather the children of God into one great assemblage. Envision these silvered messengers spilling out of the heavens into the atmosphere. You'll more quickly count the winter snowflakes than you will number these hosts. Jude announced that "the Lord is coming with thousands and thousands of holy angels to judge everyone" (Jude vv. 14–15 CEV). The population of God's armies was too high for John to count. He saw "ten thousand times ten thousand, and thousands of thousands" (Rev. 5:11 NKJV).

They minister to the saved and battle the devil. They keep you safe and clear your path. "He has put his angels in charge of you to watch over you wherever you go" (Ps. 91:11 NCV). And on the Great Day they will escort you into the skies, where you will meet God. "He'll dispatch the angels; they will pull in the chosen from the four winds, from pole to pole" (Mark 13:27 THE MESSAGE).

Whether you are in Peoria or paradise, if you're a follower of Jesus, you can count on an angelic chaperone into the greatest gathering in history. We assume the demons will gather the rebellious. We aren't told. We are told, however, that the saved and lost alike will witness the assembly. "All the nations will be gathered before Him" (Matt. 25:32 NKJV).

At some point in this grand collection, our spirits will be reunited with our bodies.

It will happen in a moment, in the blink of an eye, when the last trumpet is blown. For when the trumpet sounds, those who have died will be raised to live forever. And we who are living will also be transformed. For our dying bodies must be transformed into bodies that will never die; our mortal bodies must be transformed into immortal bodies. (1 Cor. 15:52–53 NLT)

Paradise will give up her souls. The earth will give up her dead, and the sky will stage a reunion of spirit and flesh. As our souls reenter our bodies, a massive sound will erupt around us: "On that day heaven will pass away with a roaring sound. Everything that makes up the universe will burn and be destroyed. The earth and everything that people have done on it will be exposed" (2 Peter 3:10 GW).

Jesus called this "the re-creation of the world" (Matt. 19:28 THE MESSAGE). God will purge every square inch that sin has contaminated, polluted, degraded, or defiled. But we may not even notice the reconstruction, for an even greater sight will appear before us: "the Son of Man coming on the clouds in the sky with power and great glory" (Matt. 24:30 GW).

By this point we will have seen much: the flurry of angels, the ascension of the bodies, the great gathering of the nations. We will have heard much: the shout of God and the angel, the trumpet blast, and the purging explosion. But every sight and sound will seem a remote memory compared to what will happen next: "He will be King and sit on his great throne" (Matt. 25:31 NCV).

This is the direction in which all history is headed. This is the moment toward which God's plot is moving. The details, characters, antagonists, heroes, and subplots all arc in this direction. God's story carries us toward a coronation for which all creation groans. "For everything, absolutely everything, above and below, visible and invisible, rank after rank after rank of angels—*everything* got started in him and finds its purpose in him. . . . He was supreme in the beginning and—leading the resurrection parade—he is supreme in the end" (Col. 1:16, 18 THE MESSAGE).

On the Great Day you'll hear billions of voices make the identical claim about Jesus Christ. "Every knee will bow to the name of Jesus—everyone in heaven, on earth, and under the earth. And everyone will confess that Jesus Christ is Lord" (Phil. 2:10–11 NCV).

Multitudes of people will bow low like a field of windblown wheat, each one saying, "Jesus Christ is Lord!"

There will be one monumental difference. Some people will continue the confession they began on earth. They will crown Christ again, gladly. Others will crown him for the first time. They will do so sadly. They denied Christ on earth, so he will deny them in heaven.

But those who accepted him on earth will live with God forever. "I heard a voice thunder from the Throne: 'Look! Look! God has moved into the neighborhood, making his home with men and women! They're his people, he's their God'" (Rev. 21:3 THE MESSAGE). The narrator makes the same point four times in four consecutive phrases:

"God has moved into the neighborhood."

"[He's] making his home with men and women."

"They're his people."

"He's their God."

The announcement comes with the energy of a six-year-old declaring the arrival of his father from a long trip. "Daddy's home! He's here! Mom, he's back!" One statement won't suffice. This is big news worthy of repetition. We shall finally see God face-to-face. "They shall see His face" (Rev. 22:4 NKJV).

Let this sink in. You will see the face of God. You will look into the eyes of the One who has always seen; you will behold the mouth that commands history. And if there is anything more amazing than the moment you see his face, it's the moment he touches yours. "He will wipe away every tear from their eyes" (Rev. 21:4 NCV).

God will touch your tears. Not flex his muscles or show off his power. Lesser kings would strut their stallions or give a victory speech. Not God. He prefers to rub a thumb across your cheek as if to say, "There, there . . . no more tears."

Isn't that what a father does?

There was much I didn't understand about my father's time in Maine. The responsibilities of his job, his daily activities, the reason he needed to go. I was too young to comprehend all the details. But I knew this much: he would come home.

By the same token who can understand what God is doing? These days on earth can seem so difficult: marred by conflict, saddened by separation. We fight, pollute, discriminate, and kill. Societies suffer from innumerable fiefdoms, small would-be dynasties. *What is this world coming to?* we wonder. God's answer: a Great Day. On the Great Day all history will be consummated in Christ. He will assume his position "far above all rule and authority and power and dominion . . . not only in this age but also in the one to come" (Eph. 1:21 NASB). And he, the Author of it all, will close the book on this life and open the book to the next and begin to read to us from his unending story.

Chapter 20

Heaven, Finally Home

You've been closer to heaven than you might have realized. Let me jog your memory. Zero in on your post-diaper, pre-K years. Remember your childhood? What a splendid season. Waking up was a great idea, and waking your folks was even better. The day's highlight was the first sight of daylight, and the only bad time was bedtime. You were old enough to walk but not old enough to worry. What was there to worry about? Ice cream had no calories, imagination had no boundaries, and life had no salaries. You climbed, not the corporate ladder, but the playground ladder. Life was simple. Your desires were simple. You could spend an hour spinning a coffee can or a day digging ocean-front sand. Your schedule was simple. You never checked an itinerary, consulted a calendar, or made an appointment. If you wore a watch, you wore the plastic one that came in the cereal box. Childhood has no second hand or alarm clocks. Wasn't life simpler?

What happened to the simplicity of childhood?

Time happened. Alarm clocks started buzzing. School bells started ringing. Birthday candles began increasing. We soon learned the fallacy of the phrase "telling time." We don't tell time anything. Time does all the telling: telling us to hurry through the caution light, truncate the conversation, purchase a cemetery plot. The noun *time* attracts prepositions like a dog attracts fleas. "In" and "on" attach themselves. Finish the job "in time," and get to work "on time." The demands of time steal the simplicity of life.

So does the complexity of stuff. Look at the stuff we manage. We keep cars gassed, beds made, books shelved, doors locked, and bills paid. What four-year-old thinks about tonight's dinner? What forty-year-old doesn't? You once couldn't differentiate between a mortgage and a monkey, and now your mortgage might be one of the many monkeys on your back. Stuff complicates life.

So do people. Divorces. Lawsuits. Dads who work too much or kids who won't work at all. People complicate life. They break hearts and promises, make messes and demands, and require daily feedings of grace and forgiveness. People weren't so complex in playground days. You could fight one minute and share a teeter-totter the next. In these adult days we sulk longer and bruise deeper. Maintaining a list of offenders is . . . well, it's complicated. It's been complicated ever since time, stuff, and people happened. If we could just get rid of them all.

If we could just follow the example of the Christmas tree salesman from Michigan. Each Thanksgiving he and his wife migrate to San Antonio and park their gooseneck camper-trailer next to a tent of Christmas trees and spend the holiday season supplementing their retirement income. He's a friendly sort, and I enjoy hearing about his simple itinerary. One year I asked him where he was going after Christmas. This was his answer: "I suppose we'll head to South Texas for a bit. Sometime in March we'll turn left and go to Florida." That was it. Boy, his schedule sounded good to me. My schedule had more entries by lunch than his had for the next year. Wouldn't it be great to pack it all in and go to South Texas until March, then turn left to Florida?

But we know better. We've learned better. Our complexities have a way of following us to Florida or Maine or the golf course or spa. Time pressures happen there as well. So do the stresses of stuff and people. If simplicity is what you seek, you won't find it selling Christmas trees. But you will find it by going one more round with the complexity question.

What really complicates life? Sin.

To sin is to turn to anyone or anything for what only God can give. To turn to a hard body or a Harvard degree for significance. To turn to a bottle of Scotch or a night of sex for pain management. To turn to religious busyness for guilt therapy. When we ask anything on earth to do heaven's job, we sin. And sin turns life into an advanced Sudoku puzzle.

Calculate the time we spend undoing the damage of yesterday's sin. Fighting bad habits. Avoiding toxic relationships. Regretting poor choices. How much energy do you expend repairing yesterday's decisions? Am I overstating the case when I say life is complicated today because we sinned yesterday?

Work with me on this. How much simpler would your life be if you never sinned? Never disobeyed God. Never ignored his teaching or rebelled against his will. Extract all the fights, binges, hangovers, addictions, arguments, excessive debt, impure thoughts, and regrets from your life. Don't things get simpler quickly?

Stay with me now. Multiply your answer by a few billion, and imagine how different our world would be if no one ever sinned. Work on this for a moment. If our world were sinless, how would it be different?

No unwanted babies or unresolved tensions. No nation would go to war. No tongue would gossip, no husband cheat, no wife chide. Sinlessness means no exploding tempers. Sinlessness disarms all bombs and weapons. We wouldn't bury ourselves in debt, buying what we don't need with money we don't have to impress people we don't know. We wouldn't beat ourselves up for stumbling yesterday because in a sinless society we didn't sin yesterday and won't stumble tomorrow. Or ever.

Can you imagine how sinlessness would simplify life? When you can, you're imagining heaven. Sinlessness is the chief reason heaven will be simply wonderful.

"No longer will there be any curse" (Rev. 22:3).

The curse is the consequence of sin, the hangover of rebellion. In the garden of Eden, Adam and Eve sinned. They relied on a tree to give what only God could give—life. When they sinned, simplicity caught the last flight to Seattle, opening the door for complexity to move in.

Work became complex. "Cursed is the ground because of you" (Gen. 3:17). The ground stopped cooperating with mankind, demanding "painful toil" (v. 17) and producing "thorns and thistles" (v. 18).

Relating to God became complex. No longer did they walk with God. Instead, they feared his voice and avoided his presence. When God asked, "Where are you?" Adam said, "I heard Your voice in the garden, and I was afraid because I was naked; and I hid myself" (Gen. 3:9–10 NKJV). Like a swarm of killer bees, foreign emotions attacked them: shame, guilt, and fear. Relating to God was no longer as simple as a walk in the garden. Nor was relating to each other.

Adam blamed Eve. Eve blamed the snake. The snake was nowhere to be found. Relationships became complex. And their days became numbered. Behold the knockout punch of the death curse. "[You will] return to the ground, for out of it you were taken" (Gen. 3:19 ESV).

Talk about a tumble off the side of a cliff. As fast as you could bite an apple, the earth hardened against its caretakers. Adam and Eve hurried away from God, and God set the timer on their physical bodies. The curse complicated life. The lifting of the curse will simplify it.

"No longer will there be any curse" (Rev. 22:3).

No more struggle with the earth. No more shame before God. No more tension between people. No more death. No more curse. The removal of the curse will return God's people and universe to their intended states. He will do this because of the work of Jesus Christ on the cross. "Christ redeemed us from the curse of the law by becoming a curse for us" (Gal. 3:13 ESV). Christ endured every consequence of the curse: shame, humiliation, even death. Because he did, the curse will be lifted. And because he did, life will finally be simple.

You won't sin in heaven. You won't sin in heaven because you won't be tempted in heaven. Satan, the tempter, will be thrown into the "eternal fire prepared for the devil and his angels" (Matt. 25:41 ESV). He will no longer be present to tempt us.

But do we have to wait until heaven to enjoy a simpler life? Are we destined and doomed to insanity in the meantime? By no means. You can inaugurate simplicity today. You don't have to go to Florida to find it. But you do need a Savior.

Jesus Christ has great dreams for you, my friend. He offers joy in this life and perfection in the next. Want to simplify life? Simplify today by letting Jesus forgive the sins of yesterday. "Let us lay aside every weight, and the sin which so easily ensnares us" (Heb. 12:1 NKJV). Sin ensnares us, entangles us. It trips us up.

How cluttered is your heart? How long has it been since you let God cleanse your sin? If it's been a while, now you know why life seems so crazy. Let God do what he wants to do. "If we confess our sins, He is faithful and just to forgive us our sins and to cleanse us from all unrighteousness" (1 John 1:9 NKJV).

Simplify today by letting God forgive yesterday.

Simplify tomorrow by setting your heart on heaven.

You have a friend who will take you there. His name is Jesus.

QUESTIONS FOR REFLECTION

Prepared by Andrea Lucado

PART 1

IMMANUEL

1. Who is Jesus to you? How would you describe him? What do you know about him?

2. Max explained that the word *Immanuel* is made up of two Hebrew words—*Immanu* and *El*. What does each of these words mean?
   • Why is Jesus referred to by this name?

3. In what circumstances did Jesus come to earth? Into what type of family was he born? In what type of town was he born?
   • Why do you think God sent Jesus to earth in this way?

4. Have you ever held a newborn? If so, what thoughts went through your mind as you held him or her? What did you hope for the child?

5. In Luke 1:30–33 the angel Gabriel told Mary, "Do not be afraid, Mary; you have found favor with God. You will conceive and give birth to a son, and you are to call him Jesus. He will be great and will be called the Son of the Most High. The Lord God will give him the throne of his father David, and he will reign over Jacob's descendants forever; his kingdom will never end." What do you suppose Mary was thinking as she gazed at her newborn son and remembered what Gabriel had told her?

6. Max pointed out that Jesus never abused his supernatural power: "Not once did Christ use his supernatural powers for personal comfort. With one word he could've transformed the hard earth into a soft bed, but he didn't. With a wave of his hand, he could've boomeranged the spit of his accusers back into their faces, but he didn't" (p. 21).
   • Why do you think Jesus resisted using his power when it could have helped him?

7. What did Max say is most significant about Jesus' journey from heaven to earth? (See p. 23.)
   • Do you believe Jesus came to earth for you? Why or why not?

8. Jesus came to live among us, and in doing so he experienced what we experience. Read the following verses:

At that time Jesus, full of joy through the Holy Spirit, said, "I praise you, Father, Lord of heaven and earth." (Luke 10:21)

Now as He drew near, He saw the city and wept over it, saying, "If you had known, even you, especially in this your day, the things that make for your peace! But now they are hidden from your eyes." (Luke 19:41–42 NKJV)

Then Jesus answered and said, "O faithless and perverse generation, how long shall I be with you? How long shall I bear with you?" (Matt. 17:17 NKJV)

And about the ninth hour Jesus cried out with a loud voice, saying, "Eli, Eli, lama sabachthani?" that is, "My God, My God, why have You forsaken Me?" (Matt. 27:46 NKJV)

- What different emotions do you see Jesus expressing in these passages?
- What emotions do you think Jesus would have felt while he was on earth? Can you think of passages that hint at these emotions?
- Which of these emotions do you experience most often? How does it feel to know that Jesus felt this way too?

———

9. What is something new you learned about Jesus in this section?

   • Does knowing this about Jesus change the way you relate to him in your everyday life? How could it change the way you relate to others?

PART 2

FRIEND

1. Think about one of your best friends. What makes this person your friend? What qualities of this person are especially important to your friendship?

2. Have you ever thought of Jesus as your friend? If so, what kind of friend do you consider Jesus to be? If not, what kind of person do you imagine Jesus to have been while on earth?

3. A sketch in Max's office depicts Jesus laughing. Imagine for a moment being in the presence of Jesus and hearing his laughter. How does that affect the way you think about him as the Savior?

- Think about other portrayals of Jesus you have seen. How is he most commonly depicted in art? Which touches your heart most deeply?

4. Max pointed out that Jesus was invited to the wedding at Cana (John 2:2). Why do you think Jesus was invited? What does this tell you about Jesus?
   - Considering what your relationship with Jesus is like today, would you invite him to a party you were hosting? Why or why not?

5. Fill in the blanks: Jesus said, "I came to give life with _____ and _____" (John 10:10 THE VOICE).
   - In your own words describe what a life of joy and abundance would look like.
   - Is this the type of life you are living? Explain.

6. Why does Jesus want his followers to live joyful and abundant lives?
   - Describe someone you know who is a Christ follower and living a joyful, abundant life. What characteristics or actions indicate he or she is living with joy and abundance?
   - Now think of a Christ follower who does not live a joyful or abundant life but is instead, as Max put it, solemn and heavyhearted (p. 41).
   - What similarities and differences do you see in the way these two Christ followers live?

7. Read Luke 5:27–32. Who was Levi when Jesus met him? What was his reputation?
   • How did Jesus treat Levi despite his reputation?

8. What does Levi's story tell you about the type of friend Jesus was? What does it tell you about the type of friend we should be, even to people who are different from us?

9. John 1:14 says that Jesus was "full of grace and truth." Which example of Jesus' treatment of others best exemplifies his truth and grace, in your opinion? Why?
   • What does it look like to extend both grace and truth to our friends?

10. According to John 3:16 who receives eternal life?
    • What do you think about this? Do you believe it? Do you think it's fair or unfair? Explain your response.

11. Jesus befriended other unlikely characters in the Bible. In John 4 Jesus talked to a Samaritan woman and revealed to her his true identity as the Messiah. In Luke 19 he invited himself to stay with a tax collector named Zacchaeus. To the people of Jesus' time, what was surprising about Jesus' interaction with the Samaritan woman and Zacchaeus?

12. When it comes to salvation, can you think of someone the world might view as a Samaritan woman or a Zacchaeus—someone who, in the world's view, shouldn't get into heaven?

Is there any person or any group of people that you have a hard time believing fall under the gospel's "whoever" policy?

- How do you think Jesus feels about this person or group of people?

13. What new insight did you learn about Jesus in this section?
    - How could knowing this about Jesus change the way you relate to him in your everyday life? How could it change the way you relate to others?

PART 3

TEACHER

1. Do you have a favorite teacher, whether it was a teacher you had in school, a teacher at church, or a mentor? What did you like most about this teacher?
   - What are some characteristics of a good teacher?

2. Do you ever think of Jesus as your teacher? Why or why not?
   - If you answered yes, what has Christ taught you recently? If you answered no, in what ways could Jesus be your teacher?

3. Read the story of the woman caught in adultery in John 8:2–11.
   - What is surprising about Jesus' behavior in this story?

- What do you think was Jesus' teaching strategy here?
- What lesson did he teach the Pharisees and the teachers of the law?
- What lesson did he teach the woman?

4. Matthew 7:29 says, "[Jesus] was teaching them as one who had authority" (ESV). Over what did Jesus have authority? Or what were some of his areas of expertise?

5. Max pointed out that Jesus didn't boast about or hide his knowledge of God. He shared it with us (p. 77). How does Jesus share his knowledge with us?

6. Identify one or two aspects of God or faith that you find difficult to understand. How does Christ provide insight into these things, either in Scripture or in prayer?

7. Is there a situation or an area in your life where you need to heed these words of Jesus: "Let me teach you" (Matt. 11:29 NLT)? If so, what situation is that? What do you think Jesus has to teach you?

8. Right before he began his ministry, Jesus spent forty days in the desert being tempted by Satan. Read the three temptations recorded in Scripture:

And the devil said to Him, "If You are the Son of God, tell this stone to become bread." (Luke 4:3 NASB)

And he led Him up and showed Him all the kingdoms of the world in a moment of time. And the devil said to Him, "I will give You all this domain and its glory; for it has been handed over to me, and I give it to whomever I wish. Therefore if You worship before me, it shall all be Yours." (Luke 4:5–7 NASB)

And he led Him to Jerusalem and had Him stand on the pinnacle of the temple, and said to Him, "If You are the Son of God, throw Yourself down from here; for it is written,

> 'He will command His angels concerning You to
>   guard You,'
> and,
> 'On their hands they will bear You up,
> So that You will not strike Your foot against a stone.'"
>   (Luke 4:9–11 NASB)

- How did Satan try to tempt Jesus?

9. Now read Jesus' response to each temptation:

And Jesus answered him, "It is written, 'Man shall not live on bread alone.'" (Luke 4:4 NASB)

Jesus answered him, "It is written, 'You shall worship the Lord your God and serve Him only.'" (Luke 4:8 NASB)

And Jesus answered and said to him, "It is said, 'You shall not put the Lord your God to the test.'" (Luke 4:12 NASB)

- What was Jesus' weapon against Satan? What are our best weapons against Satan?
- What does this story tell you about how you can prepare for ministry or any calling that has been put on your life?

10. Read John 15:4–10. According to this passage how do we bear fruit?
    - Read Galatians 5:22. What type of fruit do we bear when we abide in Christ?

11. What are some ways you can abide in your teacher Jesus this week? How could you connect with him in a meaningful way?

12. What is something new you learned about Jesus in this section?
    - How could knowing this about Jesus change the way you relate to him in your everyday life? How could it change the way you relate to others?

PART 4

MIRACLE WORKER

1. Max posed a question at the beginning of this section: "Do you believe in divine miracles?" (p. 99). Do you believe in miracles? Why or why not?

2. If you do believe in miracles, have you ever witnessed a miracle or experienced a miracle yourself? If so, what happened? How do you know this was a miracle?
   • If you don't believe in miracles, or if you're not sure you do, have you ever witnessed or experienced something so amazing or unbelievable that it is difficult to explain it by human understanding? What was this experience like for you?

3. Fill in the blanks: "The miracles of Jesus were not _____; they were _____. They were not _____ to his story; they were _____" (p. 101).
   - According to John 20:30–31 why did Jesus' miracles take center stage in the Gospels?
   - Do the miracles of Jesus take center stage in the way you view and understand Jesus and his life? Why or why not?

4. How did Jesus calm the wind and waves in Mark 4:39? What does this tell you about his power and authority?

5. Have you ever experienced Jesus in the midst of a "storm" in your life—a difficult or dark season that you weren't sure you would ever get through? If so, how did he bring peace or calm to that season or circumstance?

6. How did Max define faith on page 113?
   - According to this definition how much faith would you say you have right now, and why?

7. Read Mark 5:24–28. What kind of faith did the bleeding woman have?
   - Why do you think she believed Jesus could heal her?

8. Have you ever been in a desperate situation where you cried out to God as a last resort? What happened? How did this experience affect your faith?

---

9. Where do you need Jesus' healing in your life right now? In your health, a relationship, a lost dream, your faith?

   • How could you, like the bleeding woman, take a step of faith and ask Jesus for help or perhaps a miracle?

10. Mark 2:1–12 tells the story of a dedicated group of friends. They were determined to bring their paralyzed friend to Jesus. When they couldn't get in the house where Jesus was teaching, they found another way. As Mark 2:4 says, "And when they could not come near Him because of the crowd, they uncovered the roof where He was. So when they had broken through, they let down the bed on which the paralytic was lying" (NKJV).

    • Have you ever had a friend or group of friends join you in asking for physical, emotional, or spiritual healing? If so, how did that affect your circumstances and your faith?

    • If an area of your life needs healing, is there a friend, family member, or loved one who could join you in prayer? If so, could you reach out to that person this week?

11. Read Mark 2:10–12. How did Jesus respond to the paralytic and his friends?

    • How do you respond when friends ask you to pray for them?

12. According to John 9:38 how did the blind man respond to Jesus when Jesus healed him?

    • What is your first response when something good unexpectedly happens in your life?

- What miracle in your life—big or small—could you thank Jesus for today in worship?

13. What is something new you learned about Jesus in this section?
    - How could knowing this about Jesus change the way you relate to him in your everyday life?
    - How could it change the way you relate to others?

PART 5

LAMB OF GOD

1. What is holy love? (p. 126)
   - Are you more likely to think of God as loving or holy? Why?
   - Why is it important that the Christian faith involves both a holy and loving God?
   - What role did Jesus play in communicating this holy love of God to God's people?

2. Read Matthew 1:20–21. What does the name Jesus mean?
   - Before reading this section, how did you understand the sacrifice of Christ on the cross? Were you familiar with the theological concept of substitutionary atonement? Is it clear or a bit confusing? Explain it in your own words.

3. John 13:3–5 describes Jesus washing the disciples' feet. This was an act of humility and service toward the disciples. You could argue that the disciples didn't deserve this treatment from Jesus because they all failed him in some way.

- How did Philip fail Jesus?
- How did James and John fail Jesus?
- How did Peter fail Jesus?
- How did Judas fail Jesus?
- And yet Jesus washed all the disciples' feet. What does this tell you about our salvation in Christ?

4. The night before his crucifixion, while in the Garden of Gethsemane, Jesus "fell on the ground, and prayed that if it were possible, the hour might pass from Him. And He said, 'Abba, Father, all things are possible for You. Take this cup away from Me; nevertheless, not what I will, but what You will'" (Mark 14:35–36 NKJV). What does Jesus' prayer teach us about him and how far he was willing to go to save our souls?

- Have you ever asked God to save you from something difficult that you knew was going to happen? If so, what did you ask God to do, or what did you hope would happen in the face of that difficult circumstance?

5. If Jesus was afraid, why did he go through with the cross?

- Is there anyone in your life for whom you would be willing to suffer or even die? If so, who is the person, and why would you undergo suffering for this person?

- How does it affect you to know that Jesus had the same feelings for you?

6. Jesus' final words from the cross were "It is finished!" (John 19:30). What did he mean when he said that?
   - What are some unfinished areas of your life? A broken relationship that hasn't been repaired? A dream that hasn't come to fruition? What does it feel like for these things to be unresolved?

7. As you consider that the payment for your sin was made on the cross and your salvation is final through Jesus Christ, how does it affect the way you view the areas of your life that seem unfinished?

8. Galatians 3:27 says that believers "have all put on Christ as a garment" (NEB). What does it mean to wear Christ as a garment?

9. What is something new you learned about Jesus or the cross in this section?
   - How could knowing this now change the way you relate to Jesus in your everyday life? How could it change the way you relate to others?

PART 6

RETURNING KING

1. How often do you think about heaven—every day, occasionally, not at all? Why? What prompts you to think about heaven?

2. Max pointed out that while we may like a journey, we all crave a destination. Have you ever been on a long car ride or plane ride? If so, how did you feel when you finally arrived?

3. Fill in the blank: "If God is God anywhere, he has to be God in the face of _____" (p. 160).
   • How would you explain what Max means by this statement?

- What do you think about this statement?

4. Max talked about three resurrection stories in this section:
The son of the widow in Luke 7:11–17
Jairus's daughter in Luke 8:40–56
Mary and Martha's brother, Lazarus, in John 11:1–44
- Have you ever had to face the death of a loved one?
Looking back on that experience, can you see God at work
in that story? If so, how? If not, what role do you think
God plays in death, if any?

5. When Jesus said, "It is finished" (John 19:30), what was he
referring to as being finished? And what didn't end at the
cross?

6. What do these stories of resurrection—Jesus' and the others
he raised to life in the Gospels—tell us about our own deaths?
- What do these stories of resurrection tell us about our lives
today?

7. So far you've read about Jesus as Immanuel, friend, teacher,
miracle worker, and the Lamb of God, but what will be Jesus'
final title? (See Revelation 19:16.)
- What would it look like to consider Jesus as the King of
your life today? Would it change anything? If so, what?

8. Revelation 22:4 says we will see God face-to-face. Imagine
what that will be like. What do you want to tell God when

you see him face-to-face? What do you want him to tell you?

- We can't literally see the face of God today, but because of Jesus, God is present in our everyday lives. In what way have you seen the face of God?
- What would happen if you looked for the face of God in those around you? How would this change the way you respond to the people in your life?

9. Max says the one thing that really complicates our lives is sin. How does sin complicate your life?

- What would be the major differences in your life if you never sinned?

10. Revelation 22:3 says that in heaven "No longer will there be any curse." What curse is this verse alluding to?

- Considering how far back our history with sin goes—to Adam and Eve (Genesis 3)—what will it be like to live in a place without sin?
- How does imagining this bring hope to the hard or dark places of your life?

11. While heaven may seem a long way off, Jesus has already lifted the curse of sin. We don't have to be weighed down by sin, starting today. Have you let Jesus take the guilt and burden of your sin?

- If not, what is holding you back?
- Even if we have let Jesus take our guilt and sin, we need the

daily practices of confession and surrender throughout the Christian life. What sin, concern, or worry do you need to give to Christ today?

12. As you come to the end of this book, think about who Jesus was and is: Immanuel, friend, teacher, miracle worker, Lamb of God, and King. Which Jesus do you need most today? How could you commit to getting to know that Jesus better?

Sources

Text adapted and excerpted from the following sources:

INTRODUCTION
Come Thirsty

CHAPTER 1: BORN TO YOU THIS DAY
Cure for the Common Life
Facing Your Giants
Ten Men of the Bible
The Christmas Candle

CHAPTER 2: NO ORDINARY NIGHT
Facing Your Giants
Cure for the Common Life
When God Whispers Your Name

The Applause of Heaven
God Came Near

CHAPTER 3: THE WORD BECAME FLESH
He Chose the Nails

CHAPTER 4: JESUS GETS YOU
He Chose the Nails
Next Door Savior
Because of Bethlehem
God Came Near

CHAPTER 5: LIFE WITH JOY AND ABUNDANCE
In the Eye of the Storm
When God Whispers Your Name

CHAPTER 6: GRACE AND TRUTH
In the Eye of the Storm
When God Whispers Your Name
How Happiness Happens

CHAPTER 7: WHOEVER
3:16
Outlive Your Life
Glory Days

CHAPTER 8: THE CON ARTIST
Grace
No Wonder They Call Him the Savior

CHAPTER 9: HE STOOPED FOR HER

3:16

Outlive Your Life

Glory Days

Grace

No Wonder They Call Him the Savior

CHAPTER 10: ONE WHO HAD AUTHORITY

3:16

CHAPTER 11: THE WAY THROUGH THE WILDERNESS

3:16

The Great House of God

Next Door Savior

CHAPTER 12: "I AM THE VINE"

Unshakable Hope

3:16

Great Day Every Day

And the Angels Were Silent

Anxious for Nothing

CHAPTER 13: THE WINDS AND WAVES OBEY HIM

The Great House of God

Cure for the Common Life

Fearless

CHAPTER 14: YOUR FAITH HAS MADE YOU WELL

Ten Women of the Bible

He Still Moves Stones
Cast of Characters

CHAPTER 15: THE WONDER OF WORSHIP

Outlive Your Life
He Still Moves Stones
In the Eye of the Storm
Next Door Savior

CHAPTER 16: GOD SAVES

Because of Bethlehem
How Happiness Happens
Grace
And the Angels Were Silent
Next Door Savior

CHAPTER 17: "IT IS FINISHED"

Next Door Savior
No Wonder They Call Him the Savior
The Great House of God
He Chose the Nails
3:16

CHAPTER 18: THE RESURRECTION AND THE LIFE

He Still Moves Stones
Six Hours One Friday
The Great House of God

3:16
God Came Near

CHAPTER 19: THE GREAT DAY
God's Story, Your Story

Notes

CHAPTER 7: WHOEVER

1. Alfred Edersheim, *The Life and Times of Jesus the Messiah*, unabr. ed. (Peabody, MA: Hendrickson Publishers, 1993), 62–63.

CHAPTER 12: "I AM THE VINE"

1. Kent and Amber Brantly with David Thomas, *Called for Life: How Loving Our Neighbor Led Us into the Heart of the Ebola Epidemic* (Colorado Springs, CO: WaterBrook, 2015), 97.
2. Hebrews 4:16 NIV, 1984 edition.
3. Brantley, *Called for Life*, 97.
4. Thomas Obediah Chisholm, "Great Is Thy Faithfulness," hymnal.net, https://www.hymnal.net/en/hymn/h/19.
5. Annie S. Hawks, "I Need Thee Every Hour," https:hymnary.org /text/i_need_thee_every_hour_most_gracious_lor.
6. Brantly, *Called for Life*, 115.

CHAPTER 16: GOD SAVES

1. Matthew Henry, *Matthew to John*, vol. 5 of *Matthew Henry's Commentary on the Whole Bible* (Old Tappan, NJ: Fleming H. Revell, 1985), 428.

CHAPTER 17: "IT IS FINISHED"

1. Walter Bauer, *A Greek-English Lexicon of the New Testament*, trans. William F. Arndt and F. Wilbur Gingrich (Chicago: University of Chicago Press, 1979), 50.
2. Josef Blinzler, *The Trial of Jesus: The Jewish and Roman Proceedings Against Jesus Christ Described and Assessed from the Oldest Accounts*, trans., Isabel McHugh and Florence McHugh (Westminster, MD: Newman Press, 1959), 103.

PART 6: RETURNING KING

1. Sonam Joshi, "The World's Most Expensive Flight Costs $38,000— One Way," Mashable, May 5, 2016, https://mashable.com/2016 /05/05/worlds-most-expensive-flight-eithad-mumbai/#bC_o003sjgqB.
2. C. S. Lewis, *The Voyage of the Dawn Treader* (New York: HarperCollins, 1952), 213.

The Lucado Reader's Guide

Discover . . . Inside every book by Max Lucado, you'll find words of encouragement and inspiration that will draw you into a deeper experience with Jesus and treasures for your walk with God. What will you discover?

3:16: The Numbers of Hope
. . . the 26 words that can change your life.
core scripture: John 3:16

And the Angels Were Silent
. . . what Jesus Christ's final days can teach you about what matters most.
core scripture: Matthew 20–27

Anxious for Nothing
. . . be anxious for nothing.
core scripture: Philippians 4:4–8

The Applause of Heaven
. . . the secret to a truly satisfying life.
core scripture: The Beatitudes, Matthew 5:1–10

Before Amen
. . . the power of a simple prayer.
core scripture: Psalm 145:19

Come Thirsty
. . . how to rehydrate your heart and sink into the wellspring of God's love.
core scripture: John 7:37–38

Cure for the Common Life
. . . the unique things God designed you to do with your life.
core scripture: 1 Corinthians 12:7

Facing Your Giants
. . . when God is for you, no challenge is too great.
core scripture: 1 and 2 Samuel

Fearless
. . . how faith is the antidote to the fear in your life.
core scripture: John 14:1, 3

A Gentle Thunder
. . . the God who will do whatever it takes to lead his children back to him.
core scripture: Psalm 81:7

Glory Days
. . . how you fight from victory, not for it.
core scripture: Joshua 21:43–45

God Came Near
. . . a love so great that it left heaven to become part of your world.
core scripture: John 1:14

Grace
. . . the incredible gift that saves and sustains you.
core scripture: Hebrews 12:15

How Happiness Happens
. . . a personal plan for discovering joy in any season of life.
core scripture: Acts 20:35

He Chose the Nails
. . . a love so deep that it chose death on a cross—just to win your heart.
core scripture: 1 Peter 1:18–20

He Still Moves Stones
. . . the God who still does the impossible—in your life.
core scripture: Matthew 12:20

In the Eye of the Storm
. . . peace in the storms of your life.
core scripture: John 6

In the Grip of Grace
. . . the greatest gift of all—the grace of God.
core scripture: Romans

It's Not About Me
. . . why focusing on God will make sense of your life.
core scripture: 2 Corinthians 3:18

Just Like Jesus
. . . a life free from guilt, fear, and anxiety.
core scripture: Ephesians 4:23–24

A Love Worth Giving
. . . how living loved frees you to love others.
core scripture: 1 Corinthians 13

Next Door Savior
. . . a God who walked life's hardest trials—and still walks with you through yours.
core scripture: Matthew 16:13–16

No Wonder They Call Him the Savior
. . . hope in the unlikeliest place—upon the cross.
core scripture: Romans 5:15

Outlive Your Life
. . . that a great God created you to do great things.
core scripture: Acts 1

Six Hours One Friday
. . . forgiveness and healing in the middle of loss and failure.
core scripture: John 19–20

Traveling Light
. . . the power to release the burdens you were never meant to carry.
core scripture: Psalm 23

Unshakable Hope
. . . God has given us his very great and precious promises.
core scripture: 2 Peter 1:4

When God Whispers Your Name
. . . the path to hope in knowing that God knows you, never forgets you, and cares about the details of your life.
core scripture: John 10:3

You'll Get Through This
. . . hope in the midst of your hard times and a God who uses the mess of life for good.
core scripture: Genesis 50:20

Recommended reading if you're struggling with . . .

FEAR AND WORRY

Anxious for Nothing
Before Amen
Come Thirsty
Fearless
For the Tough Times
Next Door Savior
Traveling Light

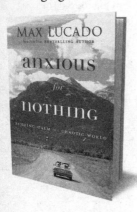

DISCOURAGEMENT

He Still Moves Stones
Next Door Savior

GRIEF/DEATH OF A LOVED ONE

Next Door Savior
Traveling Light
When Christ Comes
When God Whispers Your Name
You'll Get Through This

GUILT

In the Grip of Grace
Just Like Jesus

LONELINESS

God Came Near

SIN

Before Amen
Facing Your Giants
He Chose the Nails
Six Hours One Friday

WEARINESS

Before Amen
When God Whispers Your Name
You'll Get Through This

Recommended reading if you want to know more about . . .

THE CROSS
And the Angels Were Silent
He Chose the Nails
No Wonder They Call Him the Savior
Six Hours One Friday

GRACE
Before Amen
Grace
He Chose the Nails
In the Grip of Grace

HEAVEN
The Applause of Heaven
When Christ Comes

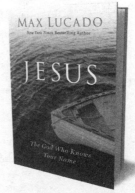

SHARING THE GOSPEL
God Came Near
Grace
No Wonder They Call Him the Savior

Recommended reading if you're looking for more . . .

COMFORT

For the Tough Times
He Chose the Nails
Next Door Savior
Traveling Light
You'll Get Through This

COMPASSION

Outlive Your Life

COURAGE

Facing Your Giants
Fearless

HOPE

3:16: The Numbers of Hope
Before Amen
Facing Your Giants
A Gentle Thunder
God Came Near
Grace
Unshakable Hope

JOY

The Applause of Heaven
Cure for the Common Life
How Happiness Happens
When God Whispers Your Name

LOVE

Come Thirsty
A Love Worth Giving
No Wonder They Call Him the Savior

PEACE

And the Angels Were Silent
Anxious for Nothing
Before Amen
The Great House of God
In the Eye of the Storm
Traveling Light
You'll Get Through This

SATISFACTION

And the Angels Were Silent
Come Thirsty
Cure for the Common Life
Great Day Every Day

TRUST

A Gentle Thunder
It's Not About Me
Next Door Savior

Max Lucado books make great gifts!

If you're coming up to a special occasion, consider one of these.

FOR ADULTS:

Anxious for Nothing
For the Tough Times
Grace for the Moment
How Happiness Happens
Live Loved
The Lucado Life Lessons Study Bible
Mocha with Max

FOR TEENS/GRADUATES:

Let the Journey Begin
You Can Be Everything God Wants You to Be
You Were Made to Make a Difference

FOR KIDS:

I'm Not a Scaredy Cat
Just in Case You Ever Wonder
The Oak Inside the Acorn
You Are Special

FOR PASTORS AND TEACHERS:

God Thinks You're Wonderful
You Changed My Life

AT CHRISTMAS:

Because of Bethlehem
The Crippled Lamb
The Christmas Candle
God Came Near

New Video Study for Your Church or Small Group

If you've enjoyed this book, now you can go deeper with the companion video Bible study!

In this six-session study, Max Lucado helps you apply the principles in *Jesus* to your life. The study guide includes video notes, group discussion questions, and personal study and reflection materials for in-between sessions.

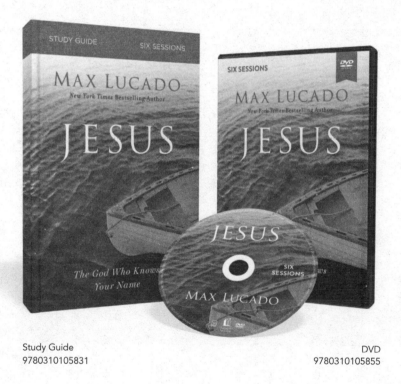

Inspired by what you just read?
Connect with Max.

Listen to Max's teaching ministry, UpWords, on the radio and online. Visit www.MaxLucado.com to get FREE resources for spiritual growth and encouragement, including:

- Archives of *UpWords*, Max's daily radio program, and a list of radio stations where it airs
- Devotionals and e-mails from Max
- First look at book excerpts
- Downloads of audio, video, and printed material
- Mobile content

You will also find an online store and special offers.

www.MaxLucado.com

1-800-822-9673

UpWords Ministries
P.O. Box 692170
San Antonio, TX 78269-2170